RISKING

IS BETTER THAN

REGRETTING

Live *Without* Regrets

CORNELIA E. DAVIS

KonjitPublications

ISBN: 978-0-9993034-6-7 (Paperback)
ISBN: 978-0-9993034-7-4 (Mobi)
ISBN: 978-0-9993034-8-1 (ePub)

Library of Congress Control Number: 2021900179

Cover design by 100Covers.com
Interior layout by FormattedBooks.com

Dedication

This Book is dedicated to my daughter Romene.

THE 3 C'S IN LIFE
CHOICE CHANCE CHANGE
YOU MUST MAKE THE *CHOICE*
TO TAKE THE *CHANCE*
IF YOU WANT ANYTHING IN LIFE TO *CHANGE*

—*Zig Ziglar*

Table of Contents

▲ Florence Italy Student year abroad 1964/65

■ Medical School summer research grant 1970

● WHO Smallpox Eradication 1975-77

★ CDC Outbreak Investigations 1979-1981

WHO EPR Centre 1990-93

SEIZE ALL THE OPPORTUNITIES THAT COME YOUR WAY

We arrived early for the *aarati (ritual of light)* ceremony, but a crowd had already gathered at the ghats on the banks of the Bagmati River in Kathmandu. The sun was setting, and I wished I had thought to bring a flashlight. It looked like all available seating on the stone-cold steps was full. But our guide marched fearlessly up the steep vertical steps and inserted the three of us, at the end of a row. The stone slab was freezing through my trekking pants. I now had a chance to look around and see where we were. We landed in the middle section of the seating. If you looked down ten rows, you could faintly detect the dark muddy current flowing gently by.

But my gaze went immediately to the opposite side of the river, some 72 feet in width before the temple. The Pashupatinath Temple is one of the most important Hindu temples in the world, only coming after the temple at Benares. This temple to Shiva the Destroyer was lit up now in the black darkness of the night. You could distinctly see the two cremation sites at some distance from each other. The *Bhatti* (priests) were still attending to building the pyre of wooden logs which held a white-shrouded corpse at the top.

1

I looked around our section of the crowd. Non-Hindus were forbidden to enter the temple, but we were welcome to visit the exterior of the site and partake of the ceremony. In my first trip to India years ago, a fellow traveler had raved about the burning ghats at Varanasi and how I had to see the Aarati ceremony. I looked around our section which had a sprinkling of tourists among the Nepalese. Suddenly there was a flurry of activity on our side of the temple. The Bhatti were bringing out lanterns and oil lamps soaked in ghee (purified butter) and other mysterious objects and musical instruments to the section to my left. It appeared that members of the deceased families and friends were seated just in the back of the priests in a reserved section for the *ritual of light* worship. In marched three priests with the sacred cord draped diagonally across their chests identifying to all their status as Brahmin. And the music started softly but then began to crescendo rapidly to a higher pitch of sacred mantras. Across the river at the burning ghats the eldest son lit the first pyre, which burst into flames, seeming to encircle the entire pyre at once. Less than five minutes later, a second burst of flames engulfed the second cremation pyre, which lit up the sky.

But my attention was swiftly drawn back to our bank of the river. A group of devotees started lighting up three large metal Christmas-tree like structures with fifty-four *diyos* (small oil-lamp) which are raised to Lord Shiva. The priests first dip the lights four times on the bottom; circle it seven times on the top in perfectly coordinated motions. The Aarati at Pashupatinath offered a devotion to the holy river Bagmati and the Pashupatinath Temple. The loudspeakers played sacred baghans and the smoke and incense from the diyos created a smoky haze and otherworldly feeling. Some of the invitees in the reserved section start a slow mesmerizing dance that I've never seen before.

I'm taken to another place and another time to Varanasi. I had planned to see the aarati performed at the famous Dashashwamedh

Ghat in Benares after I had finished my posting in India working on smallpox eradication (May 1977). I had made a vow that I would bathe in the Ganges and see the fire ceremony there some forty-two years previously. But then on my way to the temple in Varanasi, a family group carrying a corpse on a stretcher heading to the Ganges came down my street. On a whim, I decided to follow them to the burning ghats to see their ceremony. I followed them discretely, as female members of the family cannot participate in the cremation ceremony. That day, I came face to face with my fears of death. I reflected on the impermanence of life. I fought against the thought of death because I was young. I told God that I had many years ahead and I wanted to live. I wasn't ready to reflect then on it one day ending. I wanted to see the world, fall in love, raise a family, and make a difference in the world.

And strangely, there I was in Kathmandu coming full circle. You may wonder what I was doing in Nepal in November 2019. I had just finished a small group tour of the remote central and eastern part of Bhutan. I traveled to Bhutan the first time in April 2011 when it had recently opened to foreigners for the very first time. But tourists were confined to the western part of the country around the capital. At the time, that was exotic enough. Yet when I heard Bhutan was opening up the rest of the country, I knew I needed to get there *soonest*.

In my travels, I found that many remote, hard to reach places became saturated with tourists in the intervening years. Tourists change the nature of a place. When that place is similar to your culture, it can withstand the onslaught of tourists. Prices for lodging and food might go up, but the culture, at its basic, remains the same. But the same cannot be said of isolated areas with unique cultures such as Bhutan, Tibet, and Mongolia. Even if one comes as a traveler and not a tourist, you bring an outside foreign way of thinking and doing. And you bring "things." You bring the camera, the down jacket, the iPhone, and the computer. And the people you meet are excited by the new things they see and don't have, and this may cause longing and desire. I gave my leather hiking boots to the Sherpa who carried my pack on the trail to base camp Mt. Everest. My orange ski jacket I bartered for a pair of Tibetan knee-high boots on my second trip to Nepal. At the end of my journey to Tibet, I gave my old blue down jacket to my guide to gift to someone in need. And while we come in all openness to learn about their way of life, to savor the spirituality of the Buddhist way of life, the slowness of the way of life that counters the chaos of the Western life, we bring an outside culture and that changes things. Not immediately, but it's pervasive.

The capital of Bhutan, Thimphu, some eight years later in November 2019, was almost unrecognizable! Before, the typical lodging was a two-storied single extended family dwelling. But the influx of tourism had drawn many workers to the capital seeking a life that was better and less harsh than what they had living in remote areas. I couldn't believe the high-rise apartment buildings and the traffic on the roads. In the evenings, the young people jettisoned their traditional clothes which are mandatory to wear to any government structure like the *Dzong* and school or work. And they were wandering around wearing denim blue jeans and other cultural icons of the West. For a long time, the old king had debated the wisdom of bringing television to the kingdom. You can't expect a place to stay "fixed," immutable in its old ways. And for the country to survive surrounded by its neighbors of China to the north, and India to the south, finding balance would be difficult if not impossible.

But I digress. Since I was already in the area and didn't know when if ever, I would return to Asia, I thought it important to seize the opportunity to revisit Nepal. I was taking these Elderhood courses in my adopted country of Mexico and realized that my time on earth might be getting limited. The course was a time to reflect on what our individual lives had accomplished but also how one wanted to leave. Of course, no one wants to think about their death, but I wanted my ashes to be taken to Boudhanath Stupa for the burial rites of the Tibetans. But I thought that rather than just dump this idea on my daughter to figure out sometime after my death, I should investigate the ins and outs of my wishes to see if it were possible. It would make it easier in the end if I figured out the arrangements in advance. So, that was why I continued from Bhutan to Kathmandu.

That course in Elderhood stirred up a lot of feelings of the value of our lives and how we wanted to be remembered. It also prodded us to think about how we wanted to leave on our own terms. So, there I was in Nepal, and I asked my tour company to help me reach the right people I needed to see. It's interesting that as one starts to think about death, you reflect on your life. I wanted to assure myself that at least I tried to have a meaningful life. I watched a motivational speech that Denzel Washington gave at college graduation when students were on the edge of going out in the world and they had all these high aspirations. He said, *"Don't just aspire to make a living; aspire to make a difference!"*

So, it was a perfect time to reflect on how far I had followed my dreams after college and where my travels, studies, and work had led me. I still believed that I had time. It wasn't too late to accomplish additional things. Did everything go perfectly in my life? Fat chance! But it's been for the most part an interesting life and I should share some of those events. Maybe what I did and how I did it could be of help to my daughter and others.

Suddenly a blast on a conch shell brought me back to the present. The ceremony was ending. People were stirring and preparing to leave. I thought of the plans for tomorrow where I would meet a Director of an NGO who would take me to meet the head of the

Boudhanath temple. What would come of that meeting? My little group was silent in leaving the area. The guide helped me maneuver down the steep steps to the ground by the river's side. We headed back to the hotel and said our goodbyes until tomorrow morning. I wasn't ready for my bed and was drawn to the roaring fire in the bar. Only one other couple was in the bar. Ilona, a fellow traveler on the Bhutan trip, and I chose a table close to the fire and just let our thoughts drift.

"That was some ceremony," said Ilona. I just shook my head. The waiter approached.

"Can I get you something to drink?" he asked.

"I'd like a brandy," I said. Ilona indicated she wanted the same. And we just let our thoughts flow free inside us without the need to talk.

My mind drifted back to Varanasi and then to Florence, Italy, and my summer research grant to Malaysia while in medical school. What propelled me to take those opportunities? Why didn't other students take advantage of those opportunities? Was I just following Colbert, my older brother's lead, or was there something in the Davis DNA that made us want to travel? My younger brother Ed, also went off to Florence some six years later and would end up being an international corporate lawyer. I thought *I'm getting close to something*. It seemed that I was always open to opportunities. I didn't immediately think that something wasn't doable but looked for ways to go after that opportunity.

It was getting late, and the exhaustion from the day's activities was fast overtaking us. We headed up to bed and planned to eat breakfast at 7 am to be ready to perambulate around the Boudhanath Stupa the next day. But my mind was too active, and I couldn't just fall off to sleep. I went on a journey back to my early haunts.

A Year in Florence

OKAY, I DOUBT that any student alive wouldn't jump to do junior year abroad in Firenze. Initially, there weren't any language requirements for the first two years of the program since it was new. But there were other considerations. I was taking pre-med, and all the scientific requirements in that curriculum made it too difficult to depart in junior year. If you could convince the university authorities, maybe they would let you go in your sophomore Year. And then there were the costs. Remarkably, the cost of tuition for Florence was the same as the cost of tuition in Spokane. And the cost even included the opening tour of Germany, Austria, and Italy, the Christmas Tour of the Holy Land, and the final tour of England before boarding the boat back to the States! I don't know how Gonzaga was able to finagle that. Going in my favor was that my older brother, Colbert was attending the first year of the program in Italy as a sophomore. Additionally, my parents always believed that travel was educational! I just needed to convince the university organizers that I deserved to be selected.

When I found out I was selected for Florence, I was fit to be tied. I started a course in Italian to get some of the fundamentals down. We would all take daily Italian classes in Florence, but it was good to have some preparation before going. Colbert wasn't great at letter-writing, but when a letter finally arrived, Mom would relay what he was up to. Europe seemed so different, so exciting. That summer, after my freshman year, I was busy trying to decide what would go

7

into the one trunk that I was allowed to take to Florence. Colbert was to return directly to help drive the whole family across the U.S. to take me to New York to meet up with the 79 other students to board MS Aurelia, an Italian ship. Before leaving, my parents were mulling over a letter from the university regarding permission for students to hitchhike in Europe.

Our school week was from Monday to Thursday. Friday wasn't a school day to allow students who wished, to travel over a weekend. The only thing mandatory was that students had to be back in the dorm in Florence by 11 pm on Sunday to be ready for their normal courses. An additional requirement for girls who wanted to hitchhike was that they had to hitchhike with a male student from Gonzaga and that parents had to sign off on that. I had not been allowed to hitchhike in the states and my mother particularly felt that hitchhiking was dangerous. She wasn't convinced until Colbert sent her a letter stating that hitchhiking in Europe was the standard way students traveled! It was considered as normal as students taking the bus or the train, and it wasn't considered dangerous! I'm forever grateful that Col sent that letter! Hitchhiking opened up so many vistas for me. I learned to travel with a guy who wasn't necessarily a "boyfriend," to plan how to make my money go further, to see Italian works of art in churches (not museums) in small towns in the Italian countryside. I always carried my art history notebook wherever I traveled, just in case. We stayed in two-star hotels, student hostels, and surprisingly, several families offered to put us up.

I was anxious about several things. First, this class of 1964/65 was composed of juniors, and I didn't know any of them. Technically, they were in my brother's class. They would have their cliques and friends from the start. How would I fit in? I was also African American and how would Europe treat me? I didn't have time to discuss this alone with Col before I left. He returned from Europe just days before we had to travel by car cross-country to New York! And the discussions in the car were centered on Col's adventures in Italy and from the perspective of a Black male. Ever since my family's move when I was ten years old, to Walnut Creek, California, a White suburb of Oakland and Berkeley, I was always the only Black in my classes in my Intermediate School in Walnut Creek. Going directly from the south side of Chicago to be the second Black family in Walnut Creek was decidedly mind-blowing.

In addition, how easy would it be to learn another language? How would the Italian men view me? In the U.S. Black Americans were made to feel like *second class citizens*. The White majority implied that we weren't as smart, intelligent, or pretty as they were. Not that my parents didn't insist that we could do whatever we wanted. It just wouldn't be given to you. You would have to demand it. Would Europe be the same? While we students all looked forward to the "orientation" that we would get onboard the MS Aurelia, no student advisor or guidebook could tell me what to expect in that year abroad.

The Opening Tour of Austria, Germany, and Italy gave me a hint of what to expect in Florence. On the seven days over on the boat, we were greeted with a hurricane on the second day which came up unexpectedly and threw us down on the Salon floor. In the space of a minute, all hell broke out! We were tossed around and greeting other students sliding on the floor and madly being flung toward either side of the ship. The first toss caused at least three students (not in our school) to end up with broken bones!

While waiting for the first dinner seating, there was another huge toss, and we heard thousands of forks, knives, plates go hurling off the tables. An announcement over the loudspeaker after a ten-minute pause alerted us that dinner would be delayed. When we finally had the evening meal several hours later, we were led to the grand ballroom where ropes were strung the length of the room. We were passed from deckhand to deckhand and given a sandwich, and an apple and told to sit on the floor and to hang on to the ropes! The ship went through gyrations that made it practically impossible to eat and hang on simultaneously. Sometimes, the ship was perched for a minute up on its side for what seemed like an eternity and those with a loose grip went flying across the smooth wooden floor smashing into people on the other side. I made a lot of new friends that night. *I paid close attention to the lifeboat drills the next day!*

What was delightful about this student ship was that there were no "first- or second-class travelers," we were all *student class*. Half the boat were foreign students going home after a year in the States. The other half were Americans going to international school abroad in Italy, France, Germany, or the UK. Students spontaneously set up conversational classes in Italian or French to help prepare us for our entrée into Europe. When I reminisce on our travel to Bremerhaven, I'm so glad we were on the slow boat to Europe. The **Queen Elizabeth** passed us three times on our journey over. But those seven magical days afforded us the time to slowly "acclimate" to the new cultures we would find. I think to find myself rudely thrust into German culture after eight hours on a plane would have been disorienting!

Yet I was struck by how I was treated going through the European opening tour. I was like a special "hothouse flower" to be admired and treated special. On the boat tour along the Rhine river that was ostensibly to see and photograph the castles, I looked up more than once to see European tourists taking my photo or asking to be in a photo with me before a stunning castle. In Rüdesheim, I was at dinner with my classmates when a bottle of champagne was set before me. Father Regimbal, being a connoisseur of wines, excitedly said, "Connie, do you know the cost of that wine?" I responded anxiously, "But I didn't order any wine tonight!" and looked at the waitress. She smiled and indicated with her head, "The gentleman sent that to you." I turned with the rest of my classmates and stared in disbelief at this handsome guy who nodded and picked up his wine glass to salute me! I was so flabbergasted that a man had sent me some champagne! I was blushing from head to toe, although I doubt many people were aware of the blush. I graciously shared my bottle with those sitting around me. The Austrian gentleman waited for me to finish my dinner. I waited for my classmates to drift away from the table. My roomie turned to me and whispered, "Are you going to speak to him?"

"Well, it would be rude not to!" I said. And then I turned to get up and noticed he was smiling at me and motioned for me to accompany him. I was all wound up and flustered. No one had ever sent me a bottle of champagne.

He was enjoying the moment and leaned over and said, "I think you are very pretty. Would you like to take a stroll around the town? I go to school here."

I didn't know what to say. You have to remember that I was considered the "baby" of the group. I had not dated much in my freshman year. My nose was always close to the grindstone with all my pre-med courses. I stammered and said, "I'd like to do that, but I don't know you, and I'm not sure I should go out with you." But then I looked into his eyes and said, "Would you mind if my two roommates tagged along?" And he chuckled and said, "Perfect, go ask them!" And I knew it would be okay.

We didn't do anything extraordinary. He showed us the typical sites and led us by the university. We even went into a bar and he bought us all a glass of wine. I remember the feeling I had at the end of the night. It wasn't late, only about 10 pm. My roomies went up to our room. And he leaned in and gave me a lingering kiss on the mouth. *Do you remember the feeling when you do something for the very first time?* Well, this was my very first kiss with a handsome European man, and I remember it still to this day! It was only later that I realized that in Europe in 1964 folks in Germany were used to army soldiers on American bases. There would have been a sprinkling of Black soldiers, grunts on the bases. They probably had orders also about being careful in fraternizing with the locals. But there would have been few, if any, Black women roaming around Europe at that time. I can't remember even seeing any *African women* students in Paris, or even Florence the whole time I was there. Maybe Europe wasn't going to be so threatening.

During that first trip to Europe on the Opening Tour, I was just bombarded by all the new "first experiences"! First time to taste Sauerbraten, Bratwurst, or Kartoffelpuffer. The first time to fall asleep on a typical German bed with *goose feather duvets* that felt like you were floating on clouds. And, of course, our bus rolled in on time to participate in the opening days of the Munich Oktoberfest! We were given strict instructions that we needed to be back and on the bus by 11:30 pm that night or we would be looking for lodging that night ourselves. I had never seen so many drunken but playful Germans in my entire life. I never paid for even one Stein of Pale Lager as I passed from one merry boisterous group singing *"Drink, Drink, Drink"* from *The Student Prince!* And who can forget their first delicious bite of strudel or Black Forest Cake?

Not every first experience was light and merry. Not ten miles northwest of Munich was Dachau. It was an optional "tour," but I think we were all seriously encouraged to go to the Nazi concentration camp. I don't remember if we had a guide or a tour. We were free to follow the signs and to wander at will. I remember two things that stayed with me from that day. The first was that metal, arched sign at the entrance to the camp that said in German, *"Work shall set you free."* **Right!** And I remember the crematoria (the ovens). I always thought of Dachau as a concentration camp for the Jews. Initially, the camp held German political prisoners, but after Kristallnacht (the night of broken glass) the number of Jewish prisoners increased. I remember feeling grateful that WWII put an end to Nazi expansion because I knew that after the Germans got rid of the Jews, Blacks would have been high on the list to target next. Among the political prisoners was a sizable group of Catholic priests, which I hadn't known about. I suppose they must have been vocal against Hitler's policies, so they needed to be done away with. I picked up a stone from Dachau to give to a close Jewish friend who was a counselor at a Girl Scout camp in the Sierra Nevada mountains with me in the summer of 1963. I fear we haven't learned the lessons of the Holocaust given the denial of systemic racism that has undermined the American myth of "Give me your tired, your poor, your huddled masses yearning to be free!" *Yeah, right!*

By the time we breezed into Italy, I was anxiously awaiting finally greeting the Italians. This was where we would have a rebirth. Now we would finally be starting our year in Firenze. The bus pulled up to Viale Don Minzoni 25. This dormitory would be our home for the next nine months. I could barely drag myself up to the second floor and find my room. Forget a shower. I just fell into bed. The next morning the light was coming up, but I knew I wasn't in California anymore. A woman was yelling "Buon Giorno" to someone across the street. If this is Monday, I guess that means we're in Italy! We had our class schedules, and I knew what my first course was. So, life in Florence began.

What were my first impressions? Florence was noisy from 6 am to 10 pm. Breakfast was continental, which meant coffee, bread, and juice and rushing to class. Lunch was the main meal and usually consisted of four courses. *I could see I would gain some weight this year.* There was a liter of wine between every two students on the table. Following lunch was the Italian siesta for four hours. This was traditional. It was as immutable as going to church on Sundays. Initially, I resisted the pull of the bed to lie down. Then I became a true believer. Siesta meant naptime. You want another impression? Italian men had this bad habit of pinching your bum! It was annoying, bothersome, irritating, but it came under *"traditional, harmless fun"* so was protected by an unwritten code. I even got pinched going up to communion one Sunday! *Is nothing sacred? Italians spoke very fast until one day you didn't have to listen intensely to every word. One day you woke up and you just understood what everyone was saying. It took about two months.* And there was Gino's Bar right next to the school. You could always find a student to while away the time. Turns out, Italians thought I was Italian (*Eritrean*) from their former colony. I put them straight, but men still pursued me, calling, "Bella, Bellisima!" down the street.

The flower seller in the block just before our school would always give me one flower in appreciation. I missed that on returning to the states when it was more likely that the door slammed in your face because some guy didn't hold it open. Italians believed in the evening constitutional (a walk around the block to let things digest). There's nothing like an Italian cappuccino and dolce! (*And I gained 20 lbs. to prove it*).

With my student card, I had access to all museums, libraries, churches, you name it. No wonder it's so hard for some to give up their student status. When I hitchhiked to Roma, I knew I didn't need to throw a coin in the Trevi Fountain. I would be back!

Eleven Things I Learned from Living in Florence!

1. I was appreciated more *as a Black American woman outside of my country than at any previous time within it.* I gained confidence in accepting that I was taken as a human being with the same status as my White compatriots.

2. I was immediately accepted by the Italian men students in the dorm. My brother Col left word that his sister was coming the next year and they better take care of me! And they did! The very first lunch a cute Italian guy came over to the table where I was sitting with my female classmates and asked in Italian, "Are you Colbert's sister?" *Duh!* And he invited me to sit with his table of all male *Italian* students. Boy, were there jealous looks all around! I owe their warm hospitality to my making rapid headway in the language and having an easy entrée into the culture.

3. I learned to appreciate Italian wine and to not go overboard in drinking too much. You rarely saw Italians being obnoxiously drunk. They learned from a young age how to drink from within the family. Children as young as five were given a thimbleful of wine with some water added. It was a normal part of the meal.

4. Always carry your art history notebook whenever you travel. There were always hidden gems wherever you went. I was always surprised at how many Italians knew their artwork. And when hitchhiking, drivers went out of their way in many instances, to point out that in that obscure village church was a Michelangelo, or a Botticelli or a Donatello.

5. Florentini did speak Dante's Italian. The Italian spoken in Tuscany was first class. And it was easy to understand. As you went further south or north, the Italian accents changed, and there were regional dialects with structural changes.

6. Hitchhiking gave me confidence in my ability to judge the situation. I quickly learned to use my intuition to determine whether to accept a ride or make some excuse and let it go. I liked to say that during my entire year in Europe, I never waited more than ten minutes to catch a ride. I think drivers thought if you are going to pick up a stranger, why not pick someone who looked interesting and who maybe could tell a good story to help the time pass. Sometimes, male hitchhikers could wait hours before getting a lift. So oftentimes I would go up to single male hitchhikers and ask, "Where are you headed? On to Switzerland? Okay, step back." I would then stick out my thumb, and soon cars would be skidding to a stop. I opened the door and said, "Where are you going." If it was to the place he wanted, I brought him forward, put him in the front seat, and kindly thanked the driver for "taking my friend to Lausanne."

7. Crossing borders can be perilous. Try to be quick and continue the journey. Once, we were headed to Ljubljana, Yugoslavia. We got to the border late. And Jon and I climbed out to fill out immigration cards and talk to the guards. I was in the back seat and just left my small suitcase in the back. But the guards were giving us Americans a hard time, asking lots of questions, and soon 30 minutes had passed. When we came out of the guard station low and behold our ride had gone! I was beside myself. My packed lunch and clean clothes for the weekend were in the suitcase in the back seat. I was distraught. By now I was crying and trying to explain what happened. We all agreed that they probably didn't realize I had left my luggage in the back seat. I told the guards that we would be returning through this same immigration post just in case they came back to return the suitcase. But I knew that was a hopeless gesture. We would be returning on Sunday early and if they could keep the suitcase, I would pick it up. I knew in my heart I had an ice cubes chance in hell of ever seeing my suitcase again. My camera was also in the suitcase! It was with a heavy heart that I approached the Italian border on the return. When we got up to the immigration station, he looked at us and said, "Wait a minute" and took off. And he came back with my suitcase. I couldn't believe it. I opened it up and there were the stale sandwiches and my OMS Olympus camera. Miracles do occur!

8. In the end, it's best, to be honest when people ask you if you liked a certain food or beverage! When you travel, particularly hitchhiking, you need to be open to accept people's hospitality. And you need to eat what is offered, whether you like it or not! I've eaten agouti (a type of giant field rat in Cote d'Ivoire, and locusts in DRC/Kinshasa among other treats). But I grinned and swallowed it down. I was offered this drink Slivovitz- a brandy like an after-dinner drink enjoyed in several countries like Yugoslavia and Switzerland. I didn't like it, but I drank it and told my hosts "Love it!" Ten years later, on a return visit thru Switzerland, I diligently searched for the family who took my hitchhiking partner and me in and showed us around the countryside. When I unexpectedly showed up on their porch some ten years later, they welcomed me in. I immediately saw a framed photo of me and my traveling partner up on the mantle (after all those years). To celebrate, they hauled out this aged Slivovitz because "they knew I so enjoyed it." I finally had to admit that I hated that liquor and please just give me vino!

9. I had three offers of marriage in Italy. They helped me determine what exactly I wanted to do with my life. One offer was from a poor student, another was from a struggling artist, and the third was from a count who was a few years older than me. His family had money and position. But I wanted to be a doctor. I wanted to complete my studies.

10. Returning to Italy after each trip felt like I was coming home. I traveled to ten countries during my academic year in Florence, but it always felt great to return "home" to Italy.

11. My year in Florence taught me that I'm an American, but I don't necessarily need to stay in America! Although I always felt like I was an American, and I had certain American values, I didn't need to live in the United States. I could learn about other cultures and languages and live a full and independent life outside the states.

My Florence year made me realize I could live anywhere in the world. That year abroad crystalized my goal that I had a calling to be a doctor, no matter the cost. But that maybe I wouldn't be that pediatrician in the San Francisco Bay Area, but working somewhere overseas. I sometimes wonder, *What would my life have been like if I had never studied in Italy that year? But first, you have to make the choice.*

A Taste of Durian

IN THE SUMMER between my second and third year of medical school (1970), I was granted a summer research grant to work in Kuala Lumpur (KL), Malaysia. The Hooper Foundation had a space in the Institutes of Medical Research (IMR) in KL, and there was a position for a medical student to assist with the research. What drew me to Malaysia? *It was a chance opportunity.* I'm sure I had to look up the country on the world map. It was definitely outside of my comfort zone. I wouldn't be traveling with a group. I needed to find an inexpensive way to get there. And I would have to get there on my own. *You must make the choice, to take the chance, if you want anything in life to change.*

Malaysia would turn out to be both fascinating and frustrating at the same time. Three ethnic groups are found on the island. I can't lay out all the ins and outs of Malaysia's history, but in 1970, ethnic Malays comprised 68% of the population, followed by ethnic Chinese at 23% of the population, and, lastly, Indians at 7%. It would take another book to discuss how the various waves of ethnic groups arrived in the Malay Archipelago, which includes Brunei, East Malaysia, East Timor, Indonesia, Papua New Guinea, and the Philippines. One might say that Malaysia would be a type of *melting pot* due to its physical location close to other countries in the region. It doesn't matter which traditional or colonial power invited or imported the other ethnic groups; it laid the foundation for the ensuing race, class, and caste problems that exist to the present day.

Of course, the Malays were the "original and traditional" majority ethnic group. How the Chinese and the Indians came to the country and under what colonial power would determine their stature or lack thereof. Of course, I was completely unaware of any ethnic problems at the time. I just knew that I got a grant and I needed to figure out how to get to this place.

The Hooper Foundation research grant would cover most of the costs for living in KL for three months, but, obviously, I needed to find a cheap flight over. I saw an advertisement for a charter flight leaving from San Francisco to Hong Kong around the time I needed to go to Malaysia. From Hong Kong to KL, I would just take a regular flight since, at the time, travel within the region was relatively cheap. The charter was a group of Chinese Americans who were headed for Hong Kong. They had a few seats left and were trying to fill the plane. The cost for an economy seat was like half the cost of the regular airlines like TWA or Cathay Pacific. The dates of the flight worked out for me, so I signed up. When I showed up for the flight, I was the only non-Chinese on board. It seemed like most of the passengers were speaking Cantonese. My seat mates were curious as to how I found out about the charter. *Just dumb luck, I guess!*

I had an overnight in Hong Kong, and I stayed at the YMCA that was right next door to the swank five-star hotel known as The Peninsula. I looked out my window from the third floor of the Y and marveled that I had the same view of the Bay as those in The Peninsula. I knew that one day, I would return and stay there. Just not yet! This was my first time in Hong Kong, but I had no time to shop or look around. I knew I would get back someday; what I needed immediately was a good night's sleep. Early the next morning, I was on Cathay Pacific for KL. I can remember that I was slightly intimidated. Of course, the only airline carriers I knew were the American ones: Pan Am, United. I was a little unsure about the reliability of this Cathay Pacific. I shouldn't have worried. The flight was only 4 hours, but I was impressed. The seats even in economy were spacious as compared to the space we are allotted nowadays. And the meals were served on real china, with real wine glasses. My, how flights have degenerated from my experience in 1970! From Hong Kong, I had a direct flight to KL.

When you step off the plane, you know you aren't in San Francisco anymore! The humidity was so stifling. I detest humidity. I don't remember how I got to graduate student housing at the university. But they were expecting me, so I was relieved! The student receptionist at the dorm had perfect English and took me up to the eighth floor. The room was Spartan with a single bed and a study area with a desk and chair. The 8th floor was considered "deluxe" since each room had its bathroom and shower. Now use "shower" loosely, since there was just an aluminum bucket and a blue plastic cup with a handle that held about 16 ounces of fluid in the area where I expected a shower. She noted my puzzled look when I saw only one faucet. She said "If you take your bucket shower in the afternoon, the water is warm. Otherwise, the temperature is the same as air temperature." I nodded my head in agreement.

A student cafeteria was on the ground floor, and she handed me a sheet with the hours. "Welcome to KL," she said and slowly closed the door. I had received word that a student would collect me in the morning and show me the way to the Hooper Foundation.

Well, the bucket shower might be warm in the afternoon, but it was decidedly chilly in the evening. It was going to take some getting used to. But no one warned me of the muezzin call to prayer at 2 am. I'm a light sleeper, so the prayer kind of belting out from the quiet woke me up. I tried to drift off back to sleep, but the next call was at 7 am and time for me to get up. I didn't know what time zone my body was on. But the outside temperature was already stifling. Welcome to KL! A student came by the dorm at 7:30 am sharp and walked me to the Foundation. This would be my home for the next three months.

"Good morning, Dr. Davis," said the doctor in a long white lab coat. "I'm Dr. Li."

"Oh yes, we've corresponded," I replied, and he indicated that I should join him in his office. I already knew from correspondence to UCSF that I would work on the prevalence of intestinal parasites in the pediatric population among the various ethnic groups in the General Hospital of Kuala Lumpur. Also, I was to examine the load that various pediatric patients had on their entry to the pediatric ward. There was interest in determining if there were any differences in the parasites infesting the various ethnic groups. At the time, patients weren't routinely examined for parasite load but, many times, they weren't improving clinically, and it was thought that worms and other GI parasites might be blocking the meds given to treat other diseases.

Professor Li had already met with the Pediatric Director at the General Hospital, who agreed with the study. And any parasites found would be treated by the Hooper Foundation. I would be leading this research and would be following all aspects. I would head first to the pediatric ward and join the interns and residents for the daily ward rounds. The stools from all pediatric patients would be collected on the child's entrance to the ward, regardless of why they were admitted. The stools would be examined for Ascaris, Trichuris trichiura, and hookworm. The Lab would report back to the ward the findings and the patients would be treated. Treatment for the specific parasite would be provided by the Hooper Foundation. I would be examining each stool. The study would look for patterns in parasite diseases in the different ethnic groups and whether there were any specific differences.

Before leaving for Malaysia, the parasitic laboratory at San Francisco School of Medicine gave me a rapid course in identifying the three types of common stool parasites. Once I arrived at the Hooper Foundation lab, they would show me their methodology for determining if a patient had a mild, moderate, or severe load of parasites. So, I would be looking at a lot of shit at the lab! But it was a nice mixture of clinical exposure in the wards and then lab work at Hooper. At the end of my three months, I would write up the study into a mini report, and turn that into Hooper Foundation and to UCSF to justify my grant for the work in Malaysia.

There was one other student, Henry, in the lab, and he had arrived about a week before me. I can't remember what his research involved, but he was also looking at stool specimens. Henry was a Brit and he was my lab partner, so we got to know each other well. I rapidly settled into a routine. I grabbed a light breakfast in the cafeteria of the hostel and then heading for the main pediatric ward for rounds. There was a system for delivering the stools to Hooper Foundation, but if there were any late arrivals, I could hand carry them over and check them in according to procedures. One of the senior lab technicians showed me about intake procedures and how I was to examine the stools. I had my very own microscope across from Henry in the outside lab that wasn't in with the regular staff. Henry showed me where we could get lunch from outdoor stalls that were deemed relatively safe as far as hygiene. These outdoor food stalls would expose me to a wide range of Malay food.

Henry was staying with some students from London who were working in other labs at the IMR. So, at 5 pm, we went our separate ways. But on the weekends, we might decide to visit some museums or go "shopping" in the various quarters of the city. In the Malay system, the government worked a half-day on Saturdays, so we didn't have the normal weekend that I was used to in the States.

I got to know one of the Indian girls on the graduate floor (eighth floor) of the dorm. Maryam was studying microbiology and was very curious and friendly. She introduced me to the Indian culture of KL. She was Hindu and vegetarian, was as tall as me, and always wore a sari. I stood out immediately because I wore western clothes and usually that entailed cotton pants and a long-sleeved blouse. I looked Indian but not from Malaysia, so tradespeople were also curious where I was from. Maryam told me that her family came over from South India during the British colonial times. Her relatives were teachers, so she came from a long list of professionals. She told me that according to when the Indians emigrated under British colonial rule, they had work visas for select groups. So, of course, there was a lot of administrative work in the government, and because Indians were very good in English, many came over to work in the British government system. The British also appreciated the strength and stature of the Sikhs, so they were brought over to supply the military and police departments. Of course, many unskilled Indians came over to work on plantations and the railroads. So, there was quite a diversity with a resulting economic diversity.

I was surprised initially at the role of "skin color" in Malay society. Even here in the tropics, Malay high-class women walked around with these brightly colored "parasols" made of bamboo and paper to protect themselves from the sun. Even here, the women didn't want to get "dark." They did numerous treatments to keep a fair skin. And there were beauty products, both traditional and from the cosmetic industry, to maintain that charming allure. There was no way I was going to use a parasol to stop me from getting a tan. I think I had a sun hat with a bill to keep the sun off my face. Of course, workers who had jobs in the field would normally have a darker complexion than those who had office jobs. But it was disconcerting to find this bias against being dark even here among racial groups who were naturally dark.

Maryam also shared that her family had started to look for a marriage prospect for her. She wanted to complete her studies, but her mother thought she was getting too old and the longer they waited, the more difficult it would be to find a suitable husband. I found the concept of your parents picking your love interest very foreign to the Western mind. And the idea of a love match seemed absurd to her. I did agree that looking at the divorce rate in the United States didn't exactly engender confidence in the love match option. Yet Maryam loved the idea of my freedom, that my parents had agreed that I could travel and come do this research in Malaysia.

I never made a close friend with any Chinese Malays. They usually were educated in the Chinese system and while they had to study English and Malay, their English was never of the same quality as the Indians. The official language was Bahasa Malaya, but it seemed each ethnic group spoke their chosen language among themselves and used Malay in any formal situation. I heard bits and pieces about a massacre or race war that happened in the summer of 1969, one year before I arrived. Many Chinese had been killed in KL, but no one wanted to discuss it. Since I wouldn't be mistaken for Chinese, I thought it best to tiptoe around the issue and just keep my ears open.

Henry gave me his version of the events of 1969. Now I probably don't have all the facts, but the way I understood it was the following: You have three major ethnic groups living side by side. And there are some very small indigenous groups on some islands removed from KL, but they don't play a major role. In Kuala Lumpur, if you looked at who ran the business section and who were the wealthiest, then it was, hands down, the Chinese. The Chinese emigrated in different waves at different times but, initially, they came to work on the plantations in agriculture or they specifically brought an ethnic group that had experience in mining. Malaysia had significant mineral resources and they needed men in the tin mines. The Chinese were always traders and sailed their junkets to distance places, so their business sense and ability to raise funds among themselves allowed them to flourish in the urban areas.

The Malays (I'm talking about the original settlers to the islands) traditionally were farmers and lived in traditional villages in the rural area that provided land for farming. Although the Malays were the majority ethnic group, in economic terms, they were among the poorest! Although politically, the Malays ran the government, they resented that, in their "own" country, they seemed to get the short end of the stick. An election was held in 1969 that some said showed implications of the communists' hand in the election. Not sure how the Chinese got mixed in, but a call went out to the rural areas to send toughs into the capital. This resulted in a rampage. Chinese businesses and homes were targeted. There is a dispute to this day about how many perished. But the result from that time was the instigation of the Malaysian government's version of "affirmative action" that sought to bring more benefits (both social and economic) only to the Malay ethnic group. At the time I was in KL, these new laws were slowly coming up and communities were talking about them.

Although Malaysia is a multiethnic country, there continues to be an undercurrent of felt discrimination among the minority ethnic groups (Chinese and Indian). *This undercurrent has contributed currently, to a significant brain drain of both minorities to seek education, jobs, and better economic conditions outside Malaysia.* Since I worked only a short time in KL, I focused on my study research.

Occasionally, other departments from time to time would need research assistants to help in gathering specimens in their studies. It offered a chance to ex-pat students to travel to other parts of Malaysia and to travel outside the capital urban area. I went on one expedition to the jungle. The researchers were interested in collecting blood from monkeys to look for new viruses. I helped in drawing blood from the animals and labeling the specimens. So, I was privileged to see a little of Malaysia.

What I learned from my Malaysia Stay.

1. Colorism was alive and well in Malaysia. By colorism I mean the differential treatment based on skin color, especially favoritism toward those with a lighter skin tone and mistreatment or exclusion of those with a darker skin tone, *typically among those of the same racial group or ethnicity.* I was surprised to find this even in the tropics. Of course, *colorism* wasn't a new concept for African Americans in the United States. In jobs that were representative or required you working with the White majority, the lighter-skinned Blacks always seemed to be chosen over those who were darker skinned. In industries such as film or commercials, you never saw a dark-skinned Black with natural hair until recently (1990s). And the cosmetic industry made millions from skin lightening lotions and creams targeted at the Black community!

2. There is a wide selection of enticing Malaysian foods but the national dish nasi lemak, is rice cooked in coconut milk, topped with spicy sambal chili sauce. I loved Malay food.

3. I was first introduced to three new fruits in Malaysia: durian, mangosteen, and rambutans. The Chinese consider durian and mangosteen to be the king and queen of fruits because of their opposing flavors. Durian is "warming" due to its pungent smell and rich consistency; however, the mangosteen is "cooling" because of its juicy flesh and slightly acidic taste. Durian is called the *"stinky fruit"* and isn't allowed on public transport. Just getting up the nerve to taste it the first time is a feat! I liked the taste, but ignoring the smell is very difficult.

Mangosteen is the size of a tangerine but has a purple hard outer shell with the inside a white delicious fruit. But for me, I loved rambutan the most! It has a "hairy" outer shell that you have to peel off and, inside, is one oval whitish soft fruit that you chew off to expose a hard seed.

When I first decided to conduct research in Malaysia, I needed to decide if I were returning to the States directly or whether to travel to adjacent countries. It seemed dumb to be in Southeast Asia and not visit Thailand? But I was solo, and it was scary to think about how I would travel, and whether I would meet interesting people along the way. It was 1970 and women's solo travel in Asia was rare. My mother wasn't enthusiastic about me traveling solo. At the same time, a huge International Exposition was ongoing in Osaka, Japan. My dad had been stationed in Japan during the Korean War and doing orthopedic surgeries in Yokosuka. He thought anything Japanese was to die for. He supported my going on to Tokyo, and he had a good Japanese colleague who sold orthopedic surgical instruments that Dad had met in medical fairs. I asked Dad if he could contact his friend to meet in Tokyo. And if I were going to go to Tokyo then I should transit Bangkok!

The train from KL to Bangkok took two days to get to Bangkok. It was relatively cheap, certainly cheaper than flying. I would then fly from Bangkok to Tokyo and then the final stretch back to San Francisco. I got a Lonely Planet guide book to help find student backpacking hotels in Thailand and I chose to stay at the YMCA in Tokyo. Even in 1970, Japan was expensive. I had butterflies in my stomach when I thought of my travel plans. I wanted to do it, but I feared being alone on the journey. What if I found no friends? I only showed a brave front to my parents, but I was quivering inside. But here's the thing. I didn't know when I would get another chance to visit these countries. This is where you have to push yourself outside your comfort zone if you want anything to change.

On the train, you could purchase a reclining seat for the night time in a special class above the regular coach seat. My friend Maryam came to the train station to see me off. I appreciated her support. She felt it was a great adventure. She taught me the way Malaysians said goodbye. You know how we Americans wave goodbye with the arm in the air, and the palm facing the person and moving side to side. But the Malaysian way was to lift the arm and the palm is facing yourself. And the gesture is a beckoning toward you, meaning they want you to return, soon.

The train didn't seem crowded. My compartment with about 30 seats was half full. The people for the most part looked to be Thai to me. Two western backpackers were seated apart and in front of me in the car. The train was supposed to have a dining car which I assumed was forward somewhere. Until the conductor passed and clipped my ticket I didn't want to move out of the seat. There were two toilets located at the front of the car. I had a strong suspicion that they were squat ones. I always carried toilet paper or Kleenex in my purse, so I was prepared. I didn't see any solo women travelers in my car. **Great**! The conductor came around after 30 minutes. He noted I was getting off in Bangkok and told me when the meals were served in the dining car.

I like train travel. You have an opportunity to see more of the countryside. And since most of my time was spent in the capital, I was interested in the scene outside. The paddy fields of rice looked like they were thriving. The water buffalo were ubiquitous and usually had a six-year-old boy seated on it, going somewhere. I had a paperback book that I had saved for the journey. It was too early to start reading it because I would surely finish it before the trip was over, and then how would I amuse myself. A guy selling tea was slowly coming down the aisle. Yes, tea was probably better than Coca-Cola. Hopefully, one could have a beer in the lounge car. After a few hours passed by, two guys came down the aisle, looking at me. They smiled at me and I returned the smile. They asked, "Where are you from?" I replied, "Same as you, from the US!" They said they were doing reconnaissance to see how many foreigners were on the train. They thought we could go to the lounge to talk and get something to drink. It would be a long trip.

Twelve backpackers were on the train: one Swedish couple and the rest of us were solo travelers, with a nice sprinkling of Americans, Brits, and Dutch students. We decided to move forward to the lounge to introduce ourselves and then go on to dinner when the time came. I breathed a sigh of relief. I had found people to talk to and get to know. Most of the travelers were "tourists" looking forward to Bangkok. Two of the group had been English teachers working for 6 months in KL. They found it interesting that I had been doing medical research. About half of the students planned on staying in Bangkok for several weeks. Some were eventually going on to Japan like me but noted travel and lodging would be very expensive in Japan compared to Thailand, so they weren't sure about actually going to the Osaka 1970 World Exposition. The main theme of the expo was *Progress and Harmony for Mankind.*

I wasn't particularly interested in the World Exposition. I attended the New York and the Seattle ones with my family. I was looking forward to seeing Tokyo and visiting with my dad's friend. I hoped I might see a typical family home. But the first city on my itinerary was Bangkok, and I thought I should see where people were planning on staying in Bangkok. I struck up a conversation with one of the British English teachers. Brian was from London and he explained that he wanted to travel and teach English as a foreign language around the world. He thought it was a good gig. You got to learn about a new culture, made some money, and then could go on to the next country. He was planning to stay a couple of weeks in Thailand and then head back to the UK. Brian had found out the names of a few backpacker hotels and had some good tips. So, I asked if I could share a taxi with him to a hotel which was in a good location to walk around the city. I was starting to feel more comfortable about my stay in Bangkok. Brian seemed to be easy going. He was potentially someone I could visit the tourist attractions with as I found more friends at the hotel. Then we all made our way to the dining car to check out the options. I always find it best to stick with the local food. So, the Malay curry with rice sounded like the way to go. After dinner, I suddenly was feeling tired and headed back to my reclining seat which looked more like a bed now! It seemed that I had found a friend to travel with. Relax, Connie, just relax. *Risking is better than regretting.*

End of The Hippie Trail - Afghanistan

A MAJOR TRIP was looming, and it was difficult to know what lay ahead. I always get butterflies in my stomach before a big trip. But this one was leading into unknown territory. I was packing my backpack and duffel in my friend's house in Delhi. I was feeling nostalgic after my two years in India, tracking down the smallpox goddess. It was still hard to realize that I was part of that eradication effort in West Bengal and Rajasthan. Before picking up my round-the-world Pan Am ticket from WHO, I traveled around India for two weeks, searching for the ancient Buddhist stupas, trying to reimagine the Silk Road. I was quite taken with the Buddhist tenets and visited the main stupas in Sanchi, Boyd Gaya, Kashmir, and Ladakh. I was in Asia and I couldn't just hightail it back to the United States without seeing some of Central Asia. I didn't admit it, but I was very anxious about the upcoming travel to the remaining countries on the overland route known as *The Hippie Trail*. It was May 1977, two years before the Russian invasion of Afghanistan.

I was in line at Air India for the early morning flight from Delhi to Kabul. Checking in my backpack and duffel the airline check-in officer said, "You are ten pounds overweight." That caught me completely unprepared.

"I'm overweight?" I replied. I just wasn't prepared for this obstacle and at the beginning of my journey.

31

"Look, I've just been working two fricking years for WHO in remote areas in India eradicating smallpox. If you can't see it in your heart to just let me pass, fine! Where do I go to pay overweight?" She just looked at me and said, "You did an extraordinary job; you can go on."

Surprised, I just smiled and walked on board. I thought to myself that I'd have to ditch some things because I had a long road ahead.

The plane looked two-thirds full. I was the only female. I had a bad feeling that maybe this wasn't such a good idea! It was difficult traveling solo as a woman in India. What lay ahead for me in Kabul? Well, I'd find out soon enough. Do you know that feeling of going somewhere for the very first time? That excitement, fear, dread, ecstasy all rolled into one? *Kabul.* It had a certain ring to it. It sounded wild and raw. I used my American passport at Afghan immigration. It was forbidden to use my UN Laissez-Passer except in the country in which I worked. Now, I was just a traveler. I don't remember the hotel I booked. It was in the area around the university. I couldn't afford to stay in the Intercontinental. Besides, I wanted to blend in with the locals and see the real Afghanistan. I had somehow obtained a local map of Kabul in Delhi and I thought I'd just walk around and get the lay of the land. I would try to find the local tourist association and see how I could travel up to a place called "Nuristan" and to the Bamiyan Valley where the Standing Buddha, the tallest Buddha (at that time) in the world, was located. I was wearing my Indian smallpox work clothes. This consisted of cotton Khaki pants and a long-sleeved shalwar chemise (long cotton blouse). I knew Kabul was more traditional than Delhi and I would need to cover up, but I wasn't going to wear the Burqa (the tent-like covering that completely engulfed the woman leaving only the eyes exposed). The locals quickly comprehended that I wasn't one of them. I got a lot of stares. *Penetrating stares, not welcoming!* No friendly greetings like Salam Alaikum as I would get in India.

In those days, many Afghan men carried rifles around the city. It was considered normal. It didn't bother me, until I noticed that a man appeared to be following me. I was certain this Afghan man was trailing me! So, what do you do in a new, unknown city, where you don't even know the Afghan word for "help"? You seek aid immediately! I'll give you a fuller account of this story in a later chapter, but what you need to know now, is that I ducked into a fabric shop and cast myself onto the mercy of the shop owner. There are good people in the world, and they do come to your rescue. The shop owner handled the would-be stalker, and afterwards brought me a calming cup of tea. Once I was composed, he said I was only two blocks from the Tourist Office, which was my initial destination. He indicated the way, and after thanking him for his help, I walked swiftly to the location.

I quickly entered the Tourist Bureau which was completely empty. Where were all the tourists? I consulted the male attendant behind the desk. I wanted to know what tours they had available in the next week. I wanted to go to Bamiyan to see the Standing Buddha, but I also wanted to go to Nuristan. He immediately said, "There were no tours to Nuristan." I thought it better not to ask why. But they were getting together a small tour to Bamiyan in two days. Was I interested? You bet!

This area of Kabul around Chicken Street was known for its antique shops, Afghani carpets, and jewelry stores with lapis lazuli from Badakhshan. Chicken Street, which hadn't seen a live chicken for hundreds of years, had the businesses and shops and tourist places, but I saw no tourists. I liked the feeling of the area and so sought out an Afghan tea shop to get refreshed and to regroup. I was looking for a cheaper hotel than the one where I was currently. It charged USD 25 per night. Some *Aussie overlanders* gave me a tip in Jaipur. If I ever got to Kabul, go look for the Mustafa Hotel, supposedly only one USD per night. The tea house was open on three sides and had something like picnic tables that held six people comfortably. I was sitting at a table all to myself when a foreigner walked in. He was tall and lean with hair the color of bleached straw that remains in the field after the hay is threshed. It took him a second to focus from the bright sunlight to the dark interior. He looked around and then he spotted me. He walked over and asked politely, "Is this seat taken?" I smiled and said, "Now it is" and indicated that he could join me. That's how I met Carl. When he sat down, I noted that his eyes were a brilliant blue, the color of Robin's eggs.

"What are you doing in Kabul?" he asked.

"I can ask you the same thing," I replied. And for the next two hours, we exchanged the various adventures that brought us to this day and time. Carl was Swedish and had been working in the wilds of Baluchistan desert with a crew digging for oil. He hadn't seen a woman, much less talked to one for a year! His job as a roustabout was hard and demanding, but, apparently, he was paid well. But he was finished with this gig. They had struck oil and he was out of there. I related my tale of tracking down the last cases of smallpox in India and that I was taking the long road home before going back to look for a job. Neither one of us had plans for how long we were going to stay in Afghanistan. As the kebobs and flatbread were served to our table we dug into the hot spicy kebobs and let the juice roll down our fingers. I looked around the tea house. The tables were filling with Afghans (of course all male) and the light was starting to dim outside.

"I got to get going to try and find the Mustafa Hotel," I explained then called over the boy waiter to pay. Carl and I made plans to meet at the tea house again tomorrow at 1 pm.

The owner of the chai shop told me I was close to the hotel and just needed to turn left at the next winding street coming up. Mustafa Hotel wasn't flashy. It looked to be about four stories high, but one can never know about a structure until you go in. On entry, I came to the reception desk to the left, while the floor opened up on the right to some comfortable tables and chairs for lounging and talking.

I walked over to reception and enquired "Do you have any rooms available?" "Of course, madam. I can show you a room." He collected a key, and we walked up the stairs. The standard room had two single beds and I sat on the mattress to get an idea of how my back would feel in the morning. No pictures on the off-white wall and the room was Spartan but clean. He then showed me the toilets at the end of the hall. Fine, a Western toilet that was unisex with a locking door. And a bathroom that had a combo tub and shower. You needed to book the bathroom, which allowed it to be cleaned between patrons. *And there was hot water!* This was a bargain! Might not be the Hilton, but my funds would certainly go further, and I could breathe a little easier.

"I'd like to take a single room not on the ground floor, starting tomorrow. I'll be coming in the morning. Can I have a room immediately?"

"You will have an immediate clean room."

I smiled and left to hail a taxi back to my hotel on the other side of the Yama River. I liked this Mustafa hotel. It had a feeling of security and the staff weren't leery of women travelers. What a relief! That evening, I reflected on the difference between India and Afghanistan. Frankly, I was expecting it to be more draconian and that there would be more restrictions for women to move with ease through the streets. Kabul was situated in a bowl and the Hindu Kush mountains were in the distance, still snow-capped even now in May. It had a semiarid climate but the city seemed to have all these gardens which belonged to ancient palaces or were municipal parks, which made the city seem to be so green and lush. On the outskirts of the capital were orchards. The bustling markets were on little rabbit warren lanes, stocked full of colorful displays of fruits, vegetables, and nuts of all varieties. The cashews were huge compared to what was available in the states.

Make no mistake; it was a fundamentalist Muslim country and there was just a sprinkling of women in the streets. The men did the household shopping (a somewhat strange flip-flop of the Western mentality). The younger women wore scarfs over their heads. The rare woman wore the complete qitab burqa, which covered her entire body and looked like a tent moving slowly down the street. But Kabul was diverse. Bands of Kochi nomads entered the city with their camels and other livestock. And the Kochi women didn't hide their faces. The rare Western woman was tolerated. They just left me alone. That initial male stalker turned out to be an aberration, thank God. I was looking forward to moving to the Mustafa hotel but also to the upcoming road trip to Bamiyan province and an area once on the famous Silk Road that wound from China to Kabul and Herat and on to the West.

Carl was interested in seeing more of Afghanistan, so I took him back to the Tourist Bureau to sign up for the trip. Those were the days before mobile phones or messages left at your hotel. Staying up-to-date meant that you had to go back to the office to find out the details of when, where, and how the tour would be organized. The bus would depart from the Tourist Office, so you needed to get over there. We left excess luggage at Mustafa Hotel (Carl had shifted there because it had hot water), something his previous hotel was lacking.

Bamiyan province in central Afghanistan lies 130 km NW of Kabul. It doesn't sound that distant from the capital, but it took us over six hours to arrive there. Still, it's a dramatic approach to the valley, which lies at the end of a one-lane road at 8,200 ft elevation. Bamiyan was the westernmost reach of Buddhism and lay smack on the Silk Road, that famous conduit of materials and knowledge that brought the East and the West together. In this valley 1,000 years ago, a Buddhist center of prayer, art, and literature grew up. And along a vast 1,300-meter expanse of red sandstone, two giant Buddhas were sculpted directly from the sandstone. Of course, the Muslim conquest in 970 A.D swept along this corridor and the valley has been Muslim for centuries. Yet, the Buddhas of Bamiyan withstood all the new conquerors and stood as a testament to culture, tradition, and acceptance. The Buddhas had captured my attention in India and had landed on *my list of Buddhist sites that I had to visit!*

I remember we were 12 passengers on the bus, and we were to stay at this lodging that was in the valley, from which you had an entire view of the sandstone cliffs, statues, and hundreds of caves carved into the sandstone. The local Hazara villagers had constructed a series of stalls that had charpoy-like beds as found in India. We had maybe two Afghan couples who looked to be in their 30s, and then the rest were Western travelers (some might be described as latent hippies) who had been traveling overland from the West. I don't remember a "guide" at the site but a local gave a short lecture in Dari (translated by the bus driver) and then took us around the Buddhas. He also took us into some of the lower-level caves, used back in the day by monks who attended several monasteries. These caves now had been taken over by the locals and were selling handicrafts made by the local Hazaras. I thought at the time that the site wasn't protected in the normal way of a World Heritage Site. There were no guards, entrance tickets, etc. I supposed, since it was "Buddhist," that the locals saw only its intrinsic value of roping in the tourists. And there weren't many tourists then.

Our bus driver/guide showed us around the site. You could wander at will. Hundreds of small caves dotted the landscape. But this was a public site, and you couldn't worship or pray before the Buddhas. This was a *"work of Art,"* not a spiritual site.

The people who lived in this part of Afghanistan were Hazara, a minority ethnic group looked down upon and despised by the Pashtun majority group. Hazaras are said to be descendants of Genghis Khan, the founder of the Mongol empire, and the Mongol soldiers who swept through the region in the 13th century. Their Asiatic features and language, a dialect of Persian, set them apart from other Afghans, including the predominant ethnic Pashtun.

Hazaras say they are *outsiders in their own country* and have been persecuted throughout history. In the late 1800s, Pashtun King Amir Abdul Rahman Khan ordered the killing of all Shias in central

Afghanistan, leaving tens of thousands of Hazaras dead. Hazaras were sold as slaves as late as the 19th century. Those living in rural areas were denied public services. Until recent decades, few attended university or held government positions. I would say Hazaras are the "Blacks" of Afghanistan. I felt a certain kinship toward them.

Islam is the official state religion of Afghanistan, with approximately 99.7% of the Afghan population being Muslim. Roughly 85% practice Sunni Islam, belonging to the Hanafi school of Islamic law, while around 15% are believed to be Shias. This Sunni-Shia divide in the Islamic world is at the center of many conflicts. Since I'm Catholic/Buddhist, Islam has not directly impinged on my life except when I have worked in a majority Islamic country. I was passing through Afghanistan and didn't plan to stay for any length of time. At the time I was there, alcohol was forbidden to Afghan nationals. In selected five-star hotels, foreigners could buy wine and other alcohol.

Also included on our tour was a trip to Band e Amir. It is a series of six deep blue lakes separated by natural dams made of travertine, a mineral deposit. The lakes are situated in the Hindu Kush mountains west of the famous Buddhas of Bamiyan. So, on the way back to Kabul, we took a detour to the lakes. The color of the lakes was a deep blue sapphire color. We had a picnic at the edge of one of the lakes. Although it was hot outside, no one wanted to brave a swim except for Carl. I tried to dissuade him. The water was freezing but cold does not turn off a Swede. I was more worried about toxic gases, that might be in the lakes. I pointed out I didn't see any Afghans swimming. Carl stripped down to his underpants and jumped into the lake. I swear he was down there at least four minutes. I was truly getting worried that something had happened when he finally popped to the surface. He looked purple! The men helped drag him up on the bank and I handed him his towel. He started to shiver and shake to get warm. We didn't have any blankets so I embraced him so he could take some warmth from my body. It seemed he was sucking the heat from my frame. It felt like making love to a dead person that had just been taken out of the freezer. I started to shiver. Carl said he couldn't see a thing after 10 feet and of course he never touched the bottom. He told me later that he regretted the stunt. There was talk of making the Band e Amir lakes into a national park. It could be another attraction along with the Buddhas to bring tourists to the area. *Well, there can't be too many tourists nowadays, since the Taliban blew up the Buddhas!*

We headed back to Kabul. The road was hot and dusty and seemed unending. The bus pulled over to the side and we stopped at a stand. The guy was selling what looked like honeydew melons. The first bite was a cool, honey-sweet fruit that melted in your mouth. It was so delicious. I can still remember the savor of the melon to this day. By the time we rolled into Kabul and got back to the tourist office, I was exhausted from the three-day trip. We hailed a taxi to get back to the Mustafa hotel. I couldn't wait to sign up for a bath! The water was hot and the only thing I missed was having some bubble bath to put in the deep tub. I slept well that night!

After seeing the standing Buddhas, there was nothing much to keep me in Kabul. I knew I needed to get to Kenya to meet up with friends by the end of June. I planned to fly to Tehran and stay a couple of days in Iran. The Shah was still the Shah, but rumblings had started against his administration. Carl was planning to travel by local bus and hitchhiking to Tehran. We planned that he would leave two days before me. I had booked a hotel in advance so he knew where I would be. And he headed off to Tehran. What a letdown! Kabul seemed so dead after Carl left. I stuck around the Mustafa and revisited some of the antique shops looking for a small souvenir since my luggage was already overweight. Alas, no such trinket was to be found. So, I took this downtime to reflect on my nine days in Kabul.

My number one impetus for heading to Kabul was the allure of the Standing Buddhas of Bamiyan. I could sense from the lessening hordes of hippies who made it to Delhi and Kathmandu that the pull of the Hippie Trail was ending. Very few travelers were coming overland from the West. But those travelers were reporting a growing hostility, a tightening of the borders, a general feeling that maybe the good times were rapidly coming to a close. I couldn't know that May 1977 was less than two years before the Russian invasion of Afghanistan, which would bring an abrupt halt to any further travel. I didn't meet any single women roaming the streets of Kabul. Even expat men were in short supply. I'm sure I would have stayed in Afghanistan to see the Buddhas, even if I hadn't run into Carl. But I doubt I would have continued to Teheran.

The Afghan stalker threw off my sense of security. While I wasn't physically "harassed" by Afghan men, you don't realize how worn down you become from the relentless staring, the streets devoid of women for the most part, your hesitancy to smile at shopkeepers, not knowing what a smile might mean. I found the openness that I had experienced in other countries was closed down upon entrée into Kabul. Although we didn't travel as a couple, Carl gave me some "shade." No man approached too close; no man dared to follow us. We sat together on the tour bus, we shared the limited lodging available at Bamiyan, we ate together. It just takes more effort to travel as a solo woman in fundamentalist Muslim countries. It's so draining. I wouldn't realize how draining until I was posted to Pakistan some four years later. Yet, I was drawn to Afghanistan. I loved the wide, open places in the mountains and the rugged semi-arid land. I wanted to learn Dari and make contact with the women and find out what their dreams were. I wanted to return one day and work to improve the health of women and children. I never got the chance! War intervened.

I could sense that this was the end of the road for me in Central Asia. I would travel part of the overland route and touch down in Iran. But my goal was looking far ahead. Now I needed to get to Kenya to rendezvous with friends who studied with me in medical school and residency. When I accepted a posting in India with smallpox eradication, they accepted positions to teach in the Nairobi School of Medicine. We kept in contact all throughout this time and I was to arrive in Nairobi before they left for home leave back to Oregon, if I wanted a place to stay in Kenya. I focused not so much on seeing the sights in Iran, but to use it as a way station to figure out the best and quickest route to Kenya. Anyway, I knew on arrival I would have at least one friend in Tehran!

The Last Plane to Nairobi

❦

THE BEAUTY OF having a Pan American Round the World ticket was the ease of booking flights and the knowledge that Pan Am had this extensive routing to places *off the beaten path*. And if they didn't fly there, it was easy to transfer that leg of the ticket to other carriers on the routes because of the intrinsic value of the Pan Am ticket. When I initially made plans to pass through Afghanistan, I wasn't sure if I wanted to fly directly to Nairobi after Kabul and not make any other stops. After I met Carl, I thought it would be fun to meet up in Tehran and see the Peacock Throne and then head immediately to Kenya. That was the plan. I gave Carl the name of a three-star hotel where I had reservations. He was to call me on the day I arrived. In the meantime, he was going to stay in some backpackers' hostel in the city. That was the plan.

It was a short flight to Tehran, and I was grateful that I wasn't on the road for two days. I hoped that Carl had arrived with few problems. He called a few hours after my arrival and came to the hotel. We quickly made plans to visit the following: the Golestan Palace with the famous Peacock Throne, the National Museum of Iran, and other sites. *It was strange being in Tehran.* I'm not sure I would classify Tehran as a *beautiful* city, but the Alborz mountains were a stunning backdrop against the blue sky. Tehran was immense and chaotic compared to Kabul; and it necessitated getting used to another language, Persian.

I wanted to visit Golestan Palace to see the Peacock Throne in the Mirror Room building of the palace. At the time, I never understood why I saw no peacocks anywhere on this platform that looked like a sun with radiating disks. Only now, 43 years later, I find I had a fatal misunderstanding of what I saw that day. The famous Peacock Throne commissioned in the early 17th century by emperor Shah Jahan and originally located in the Red Fort of Delhi was looted by Nader Shah, the emperor of Iran. Nader Shah may have won the war, but the throne never made it back to Persia. History is opaque about what happened, but the jewels were lifted from the throne and eventually wound up in various *state crowns* around the world. What I saw in the Mirror Room at Golestan Palace that day was something referred to as the *Sun Throne*.

The so-called Peacock Throne currently on display outside the vault door in the Iranian Treasury is the throne ordered by Fath Ali Shah in 1798. Taking a daybed-style Takht (table in a teahouse), they adorned it with an extravagantly carved sun, studded with 26,733 precious stones. Before long, it became known as the Sun Throne. Later Fath Ali married Tavous Tajodoleh, nicknamed *Tavous Khanoum* or Lady Peacock, and the throne became known as the Peacock Throne in her honor. But it's really the Sun Throne. Okay, you probably could care less, but I finally understood why it had no peacocks! That day, Carl and I saw a lot of gilded buildings and stunning halls of mirrors so we can be forgiven in confusing certain facts of history.

Before going on to visit other historical sites, I begged off to go to the Pan Am office to make ongoing flight plans. Much to my dismay, I was informed that Pan Am had discontinued the route through Tehran and I suddenly found myself without an easy way to get out of Tehran (without hitchhiking out). I then spent the next two days in a frantic search to beg, borrow, or steal my way out of Iran. Remember, this is before the internet, and "just google it" or pick up a mobile phone to call Pan Am headquarters. Suddenly, my priceless Pan Am ticket was worthless. I wasn't enthusiastic about purchasing a brand-new ticket. Other airlines were full capacity on the days I was trying to leave the capital, and I was reduced to crying. Someone finally mentioned El Al airlines, Israel's national airline.

Now, I don't know about you, but my normal inclination isn't to choose an Israeli plane to leave the capital of a Middle Eastern Arab country. But hey, I was desperate to leave. So, I found the airline's office. Before entry, I had to show the photo page of my passport outside the building, to the camera. The door opened into a small foyer where I had to again, hold up the passport to another camera for them to verify that I was American. Only then was I allowed inside. There were guards with guns, and I had a bad feeling again, in the pit of my stomach. Maybe I didn't want to take this plane anywhere. Now, at the time, El Al was the only commercial airline to equip its planes with missile defense systems to protect against surface-to-air missiles. It was considered one of the world's most secure airlines, thanks to its stringent security procedures, both on the ground and onboard its aircraft. Although it has been the target of many attempted hijackings and terror attacks, only one El Al flight has ever been hijacked; that incident didn't result in any fatalities.

An airline representative told me that the most direct way to Nairobi from Tehran on one of their flights was to fly to Haifa, layover there and go on to Nairobi. They had a plane leaving tomorrow. And they would accept the Pan Am ticket leg of the trip for their route. I signed right up! I had a hurried meet up with Carl to explain my sudden change of plans. I thought I should get out while the getting was good. It was an abrupt and hurried end to our rendezvous in Tehran. Carl was eventually heading back to Sweden. We talked briefly about him meeting me again maybe in London before I headed back to the States. I had made a reservation at this hotel in London and I knew I had to be there by a certain date. My six months journey would be rapidly drawing to a close. It all felt so haphazard and quick. It wasn't the departure that I had planned. I only had the name and telephone number of the hotel, which I gave to him. *Fat chance we would ever meet again.*

So, I surveilled my belongings to see what objects I might be able to put in my "purse" to lighten the luggage that would be checked. I was hoping to avoid the Delhi confrontation. Then I tried to take a "nap" since I would be leaving at some ungodly hour like 1 in the morning. I wasn't feeling well. It's not Delhi belly, and I didn't have a high fever and chills which might predict malaria. I was tired. True, I had my period, which now had lasted more than 14 days. It was very unusual for me because my periods were short and sweet; never more than three days and no cramps. I wasn't sure what this change meant. It would be good to get to Kenya and just relax with my friends. I was going on two months of being constantly on the move, and I probably needed just to slow down.

Tehran in the daytime is a kaleidoscope of movement and noise. So, I was unprepared for the silence of the road at midnight. No taxis, trucks, bicycles, or animals were on the boulevards. I had calculated an hour to get to the airport. But with no traffic, it was a breeze. There was no hassle with the luggage, and once we boarded, I fell asleep. I didn't wake until the pilot announced that we were approaching Haifa. It had been more than a decade ago since I last visited Haifa on the Christmas tour of the Holy Land during my year-long stay in Florence. I wondered what it was like now. I had a twelve-hour layover and I wanted to get a room and lay flat on a bed. I was feeling dizzy, so I felt it best to get a hotel room and not sit in the airport for that length of time. The plane landed some distance from the airport. And several Israeli soldiers boarded the plane and proceeded to intently inspect each passenger as if they were looking for a particular person. Then the chief steward announced that we could deplane. As we each descended the plane, we were inspected again before boarding the bus for the airport terminal.

What's more, I wasn't feeling chipper, and once in the terminal, I verified when my ongoing flight would depart some twelve hours later. I went back to immigration and I asked the officer if I could leave the airport and find a hotel close by.

"I'm feeling dizzy and I need to lie down, so I think its best if I go to a nearby hotel," I said.

He looked at my onward boarding card and he said, "You will have to give me your passport," and he filled out an orange card on which he added my passport number and date of expiration. "Return to the airport in ample time to go through procedures. Give them this card, and you will get back your passport."

All I could think about was getting to a clean hotel and lying down to sleep. I collected my luggage and exited the airport. There was a taxi stand right out front and the taxi guy spoke English. "I have a short layover, and I want to go to a nice hotel that is close to the airport," I said.

"No problem madam," he said. "I know one very close."

In less than 15 minutes, I was in front of a hotel. The bell boy came out and helped me with my luggage. The taxis guy took USD 2 and I was at the reception desk. I explained to the guy behind the desk that I needed to be back at the airport in nine hours. I was feeling dizzy and didn't want to go out for food. I asked if I could order something to be delivered up to the room?

"No problem madam." I told him the airport had my passport and showed him the card. I would pay for the room with a credit card, which he said was fine. And the bell boy took me to the room. I ordered kebobs and some soup with a nan-type middle eastern bread and I collapsed on the bed. I took out my alarm clock and set it. The food came almost immediately and after scarfing it down, I fell off to sleep. It felt good to lie flat. I figured I would take a shower before returning to the airport, and I fell into an uneasy sleep. In no time the alarm went off and I hopped up. A quick shower woke me up and I descended to the ground floor to ask the receptionist to call a taxi to return me to the airport.

"I hope you had a pleasant stay," said the man, and I was off to start the next leg of the journey. The Haifa airport was now bustling and there was a line to enter the airport. When I came up to the first checkpoint the soldier asked me for my passport. So, I looked in my purse, handed him the orange card, and explained that I went to a hotel, but did he know where I was to go to collect my passport? *And then started the next three hours of a "Twilight Zone" episode from Hell!*

"You don't have your passport?" the soldier demanded. "You left the airport?"

I explained again that I had been very sick and had asked immigration to leave the airport to go to a hotel. I had to give up my passport. Then the interrogation began: "Who are you? Do you have another piece of identification? Which hotel did you go to?" I was starting to get anxious now. "I don't know the name of the hotel, but it's close, less than 15 minutes away. He called another security guard over to discuss in Hebrew. This guy was sterner. "You don't know where you stayed?"

I said I was sick. "Wait. I keep all my receipts because at the end of this trip I have to turn all receipts in to get reimbursed." I dumped my purse out on the floor and finally found the hotel receipt and the younger guy went off with the bill. The older guy said, "Open up your luggage!" "Right here in the middle of the hall?" We weren't near any of the booths to sign in to El Al flights. So, I bent down to unlock my duffel and he started pulling out clothes and ransacking through my items.

"Hey, buddy, what are you doing?"

The other soldier returned and said, "The hotel said that a woman came in and was sick and stayed in her room all the time. They brought up food and then after 8/9 hours she left for the airport." He shoved the orange card in my face and demanded "Why did you give up your passport"?

"Because a soldier with a rifle said if I wanted to go out, I had to do this exchange."

"Are you sure you don't have another piece of identification?"

"Well, yes I have a UN laissez-passer passport (LP) but it's only to be used in the country of service, which was India." And I searched in my backpack to find it. He went to take it, and I said, "I'm not giving it to you. Wherever you are planning to take this, I'm going also. I'm not giving this up! Hey, you pulled my stuff out of my duffel so just wait and help me get it in." Then he dragged the bag behind the security desk, and I followed. We went through some closed security doors that needed special cards to open them and then descended into the bowels of the airport down two or three flights of stairs. It was very scary until we came to a room that had about 60 TV screens stuffed in it and three or four men intently looking at the security cameras. One official turned around and came over. He smiled and said, "I was wondering when you would show up."

He took my LP book and looked at the data and then handed it back to me. Then he went over to a series of open bookshelves to retrieve where they had stashed my passport. He took my orange card and said, "Never give up your passport!"

And he finally handed me back my American passport. "You left the airport and went to a hotel on the Arab side of Haifa."

"This orange card is just to let you easily pass around the inside of the airport, but you should have never left the airport."

I started to tear up and said, "I was sick yesterday and needed to lie flat. I could only think of going to a hotel. The guard didn't say anything about not leaving the airport!" And then I looked at the clock on the wall. "Crap, my plane is supposed to leave in 20 minutes; I got to make this connection please?"

He said, "I have them holding the flight for you." One of those airport golf carts arrived with additional soldiers, and my luggage and I piled into the cart. Then he smiled and said, "Have a nice trip!" We sped to the tarmac and raced to the plane. They had already hauled back the flight stairs leading up to the cabin. The door was still open and a stewardess was at the entry as they dragged the stairs back. Some luggage guy took my bags to the back underbelly. And I ran up the stairs. Everyone on the plane stared at me as if I were some terrorist who was being kicked out of the country. I sank into my seat and closed my eyes and breathed a long sigh of relief. *Thank you, God, for helping me get back my passport and letting me make this flight! I promise never to let my passport out of my sight ever again!* And to this day, I have never again *willingly* given up my passport. I counted myself lucky. Once again, I was profiled. I looked like I could be Arab. I had gone straight to the Arab section of town and disappeared. I couldn't initially tell the Israelis the name of the hotel. They called the hotel who verified my story. When the Israelis do security, they do thorough security. They pulled everything out of my duffel. I barely made my flight. I didn't wake again until the pilot announced we were approaching Nairobi, Kenya, and would soon be landing. Soon, I would be seeing my friends in Nairobi.

Nairobi was a welcome sight. Since it was a British colony, everything worked like clockwork. The accents changed and were very British. Kathy and Bob had sent me explicit directions on how to get to their house because they had been given university housing, as they were teaching in the medical school.

I was tired and hot, and needed a bath and couldn't wait to see my friends. We drove down a neat street of identical houses. It was about 1 pm and no one was out on the street. I guessed people were at the university or the hospital. The taxi guy got my luggage and took it up to the door. He said, "Are you sure this is the address?" "Yes, this is fine, you can leave me." And I rang the doorbell. No response. The curtains were closed, and I started to get this bad feeling. Where were my friends? Had I messed up the timing about when I needed to arrive? There was a bench on the front porch, and I slumped down, placing my backpack and duffel at my feet. *Ok, what was Plan B?* I hadn't planned on staying in a hotel. And my wallet hadn't planned on it either! A car drove up to the neighbor's house across the street. A white man got out and went up the steps. He turned back to look at me, and then opened his door and went in.

It looked like Plan B was to go knock on the neighbor's door and see if he knew anything. Crap, this wasn't going to be fun. So, I loped across the street and rang the bell. The guy came to the door and I said, "Hi, I'm a friend of Bob and Kathy (we went to medical school together). I was working in India and I was passing through to meet them. I was supposed to get here this week. But it seems like they aren't here."

He said, "They said something about going to the coast. But I did see Bob this morning going to work." "OK, I'll just wait on the front porch for a little while longer, and then I'll be off." *At least the neighbor wouldn't call the police on me, I thought.* And I returned to my guard seat on the bench and waited. Eventually, down the street came a white Toyota Landcruiser that drove up the driveway. And out jumped Bob!

"Connie! We were wondering when you would show up. We wanted to go to the coast for 2 weeks before leaving on home leave but didn't know when you would finally show up. Kathy left with Kevin, our son, two days ago for the coast. I was hoping you would show up in time so you could join us!"

"Well, finally, I have some luck!" And I launched into my adventures in Afghanistan and Iran. Bob dragged my luggage into the house and said," Take a shower quickly because we are booked on the night train to Mombasa and we need to leave for the train station in one hour." The next thirty minutes flew by and he called for a taxi. We waved to the next-door neighbor who seemed delighted that we had found each other! And we were off!

Bob explained on the way to the train station, that Kathy and Kevin, and the ayah (nanny), and Kathy's brother John Wiley, had left on the train earlier in the week. They had rented a beach house in Mombasa and went ahead to settle in. Bob planned to work until Friday and then come down on the train. They were hoping against hope that I would arrive on time. He had reserved a first-class sleeping compartment for himself and the missus. *There might be a slight problem with me posing as his wife, since this was the White first-class compartment!* "I'll let you do all the talking!" And soon we were at the Nairobi train station. I've always loved travel by train since moving across the U.S. from Chicago to California on the famed *California Zephyr* when I was a kid.

Certain trains attain legendary status that attract people like iron nuggets to a magnet. *Well, the Nairobi-Mombasa meter-gauge single-track train is one of those legends.* I heard stories about the line, and I was excited that I actually would be traveling on it. Back in the 1800s during the Scramble for Africa among the various colonial powers, the UK's imperial agenda was to thwart French east-west designs in Africa by building a railroad to connect British colonies in East Africa. It envisioned connecting the port of Mombasa (gateway to the Indian Ocean) to the landlocked protectorate of British Uganda and create a railroad juncture and headway in a place called Nairobi. A railroad engineer George Whitehouse who had built railroads around the world was commissioned for this feat. *If he had known about the tropical diseases, the tribal hostilities, the raging rivers, and deep ravines, the man-eating lions of Tsavo, not to mention the eventual exorbitant costs, I doubt he would have accepted the job!* British Parliamentarians at the time ranted about the costs even before they occurred and named the track "train to nowhere" and eventually *"the Lunatic Line."* If you remember the opening scenes of the film *Out of Africa*, the expanse of the rolling savanna teeming with wildlife, that was my experience in 1977. But I'm getting ahead of my story.

The Nairobi Railroad Station was a Victorian structure out of Dickens time. Bob went to collect the reserved tickets. We were thirty minutes early and just walked around the area taking in the antique lamps and fixtures from a bygone era. The overnight train was scheduled to leave the station at 7 pm sharp and pull into Mombasa at 7 am. The train pulled in from whatever siding it had been on, and we went looking for the first-class sleeper compartments. It was like walking into another era. The compartment seemed spacious with huge dark brown couchettes that folded down into beds. The Kenyan porter came into the compartment and in perfect British English announced that when we went for dinner, he would turn down the beds. And the conductor would be by shortly to check the tickets. I rolled my eyes at Bob and when the porter left, I said, "I'll let you deal with the conductor. I will be engrossed in my book! Or pretending to be asleep." Then we heard the whistle blowing, felt a mighty pull forward, and chugged out of the station exactly on time.

It takes some time for the train to get to the outskirts of Nairobi. You go through the Kibera slums before you finally see the savanna. The train's speed isn't fast, so you have ample time to watch life roll by. African mothers are preparing meals over an open fire, kids are kicking a soccer ball, and it's already dark since we're at the equator. Bob went out to waylay the conductor before he entered the compartment. He came back in with a satisfied grin on his face and stated, "It's taken care of, no problem." *So, I guess I won't be kicked out of First Class!*

"I'm starving," I say. "Let's head for the dining car now and beat everyone!" And we headed out. It was just two cars ahead. The dining car looked like it was from the 1930s. It had pristine white linen tablecloths and china from the bygone days of the railroad and real silver service. I was impressed. The waiter came over and presented the selection for the fixed menu. We started with a delicious creamy potato and leek soup, followed by a selection of curries, and some kind of pudding for dessert. *Okay, in my mind, the Brits don't do dessert all that well, but we were washing everything down with my favorite Kenyan beer, Tusker!*

When we arrived back to our compartment, the beds were turned down. The temperature in the cabin was lovely with the air conditioning. I couldn't see anything now outside, but there was just the gentle roll of the car, tumbling down the tracks. I was exhausted from having just made it on this trip to Mombasa. I couldn't keep my eyes open, so I said goodnight to Bob, brushed my teeth hurriedly in the sink, and fell off to sleep before my head hit the pillow. Morning came early and, in the distance, I could see a herd of giraffes galloping. Then I knew I was in Kenya when I saw the wild animals out the window. Bob was still asleep, so I didn't shout when I saw hundreds of wildebeests! I was hooked. I could live in this Kenya. I quietly got up and looked at my watch. It was 6:30 am. I quickly brushed my hair and tried to tidy up and smooth my wrinkled clothes. Bob was up now and said, "We're almost through Tsavo National Park. If we hurry, we can get breakfast and some coffee before we pull into Mombasa." And we were off to the dining car!

I could feel the temperature difference already between the cool of Nairobi and the impending heat and humidity of Mombasa. I better get used to it. Bob regaled me about all the parks he and Kathy had visited since arrival in Kenya two years ago. He mentioned Kathy's brother was also visiting and had a trekking proposal for me. There was some little hitch to me trekking up Kilimanjaro in Uganda, but he'd let Kathy explain. *Uh, seems I might not be trekking to Kili?*

We hurried back to our compartment and made sure we had all our luggage ready to go. We were fast approaching the station. Bob pulled down the window so we could lean out and try to spot Kathy on the platform. More likely, she would spot us first! *I'm surprised they let people come on the platform to greet friends, but TIA (This is Africa).* And then I heard someone yelling, "Davis, Davis you made it!" Kathy was holding a nine-month-old baby with blond hair in her arms.

I yelled back, "Did you think I was going to miss a trip to Mombasa?" And we piled out of our air-conditioned room, onto the train platform, to be hit with a blast of furnace-hot air bathed in 1,000% humidity (or at least it felt that way). It was 5 years since we graduated from medical school at UCSF in 1972. Kathy took a residency in the state of Oregon because her husband was doing a residency there. And I headed to USC-LA County Hospital for a pediatric residency. We initially kept in contact because we had formed a tight clique of three women in med school. I wondered briefly whatever became of Betty. There were only five women in our class, and the three of us bonded immediately on the first day! Who could imagine that we would meet up again, thousands of miles from the States in Kenya? And we took off together, not letting the other get a word in. Bob was left holding baby Kevin.

They had rented this idyllic cabana some kilometers out of the congested city of Mombasa. You could walk out the front door and you were on the beach. Fishermen would bring their catches to sell around the back of the house. There is nothing like freshly caught fish, not one hour old. Shrimp, lobsters, crabs, marlin, you name it! We rarely ate red meat! The bungalow was packed, since Kathy's brother John was there, the ayah for the baby, and we three adults. *It took days to catch up on our lives over the years.*

"So, what's this about my *not* climbing Mt. Kilimanjaro? I thought I was joining a South African group to go up."

"Well, Kenya had a falling out with Tanzania and Uganda over their *East African Union*. Now, if you drive over the border to Uganda in our Landcruiser, the authorities will not let it return. Some falling out over customs, duties, money! And as much as we love you, Connie, we need our Toyota Landcruiser. So, John, Kathy's brother, was looking for a partner to climb Mt. Kenya. It's a quick but brutal climb. There are porters. *Okay, it doesn't have the same caveat as Kilimanjaro.* "Few people get altitude sickness because you are coming down as soon as you reach the top," said Kathy. I could sit there and pout, or I could count myself lucky that I had a trekking partner. Let the adventure begin! I climbed Everest in Nepal, and I wanted to climb the highest peak in Africa, but that's life. *I'll just have to settle for the second highest peak in Africa!*

That evening, as I drifted off to sleep sharing the room with the baby, it was hard to get a handle on where I had been on the first of June. I saw the tallest standing Buddha in the world at Bamiyan. Got the last plane out of Tehran after seeing the Peacock Throne (which turned out to be the Sun Throne). I almost didn't get out of Haifa. Turned up at the house in Nairobi after everyone save Bob had left for the beach. *I just missed a potential disaster by one day.* But now I was laughing in Mombasa, wearing a bathing suit that would surely get me stoned in Afghanistan, and in five days would be climbing the highest mountain in Kenya. Life was an adventure. *Just be open to opportunities!*

RISKING CAN BE
DANGEROUS

I know the previous chapters gave you a taste of what you can experience if you open yourself up to opportunities. They can be exciting, exhilarating, stupendous, and uplifting, but there's always another side to the light. It can be dangerous! Yet, sometimes, the danger is worth the risk! How do you determine what risks to take? I suppose the answer might be different for different people. I've always had a keen sense of intuition. What is intuition? It's when you have an instinctive feeling rather than conscious reasoning. On a certain level, it's a "gut" feeling that's understood immediately. I'm not sure how you develop it, but you need to trust the feeling and go for it.

In my first memoir, **Searching for Sitala Mata: Eradicating Smallpox in India**, we junior doctors in our orientation were strongly counseled to work within the borders of India. We were explicitly told not to cross international borders. But when I was faced with a rumor that smallpox cases were just across a nebulous border and knowing that in previous years smallpox was reintroduced into the state of West Bengal by folks coming from Bangladesh, I knew instinctively the risk was worth it. India was so close to eradication, and outbreaks in all of India were in single digits. I needed to know for sure and conduct containment activities on the Indian side of the border if smallpox were present. I was willing to go against orders to prevent a reintroduction and an explosion of cases on our side. I went across the border with my team. We located the concerned village and in fact, there were eight cases of smallpox in one family. We immediately returned to India and commenced ring containment and vaccinated everyone within a one-mile radius. Smallpox could have easily been reintroduced by relatives or close friends going across the border for trade. *So, for me, the risk was worth it!*

When I traveled to Afghanistan right after my time in India eradicating smallpox, I knew it was very different even from India. Practically the whole population practiced a fundamentally conservative Muslim faith. All women were in purdah, a state of seclusion or secrecy. If a woman went outside with a male relative, she would normally be completely veiled, covered by a burqa, an all-enveloping covering except for the eyes. An Afghani woman never went outside alone. She would have, at the very least, a five-year-old son with her. So, I knew I would be pushing the envelope and the cultural norms, and that it wouldn't be comfortable. But I wanted to see the standing Buddhas of Bamiyan. I was willing to risk the uneasy feeling in my gut, for the chance to see this World Heritage site. I didn't think I would be in any physical harm, just a bunch of men staring at me. So, I was willing to take the risk.

When folks travel outside their country, they know they'll face many minor risks such as food or water that might be contaminated and cause gastroenteritis. Everyone knows of "Delhi belly," laughs about it, and shrugs it off. You carry Imodium to stop diarrhea and you know not to drink the water! This is considered a minor risk of travel to foreign places and is an accepted risk. However, few people would go into a country that was having a full blown "cholera" outbreak because that can kill you.

I think at times, the risk is worth it. But there's no excuse for willfully ignoring the danger. Ignorance is no excuse for leading others down a pathway of destruction. Silence is just complicity when you know something is deadly wrong and you say nothing! So, this section shows how I weighed the risks and had my eyes wide open.

Stalker Alert- Afghanistan

I WANT TO encourage women to do what they desire in terms of education, of looking for adventure, of pushing the boundaries. But there are inherent risks in trying to be independent in what is still a man's world. My brothers going off to Florence, Italy and hitchhiking didn't present the same risks that I as a woman had. That provoked the precautions the university tried to instill. Even traveling with a male partner doesn't ensure your safety. But oh, the things one will miss by playing it too safe. While you're bound by the physical location of where your mother was when you were born, it doesn't mean that you can't explore beyond that city, state, or country. Know the risks, weigh the costs, but go out to see the world.

I gained confidence working in smallpox eradication in India, and I worked at the lowest level, in the field, under trying circumstances, long hours, dealing with caste and class rules that would drive anyone crazy. But I was always with my team, which, for me, was my "family." They were my protection against the world. When I decided I wanted to visit places in India where I wasn't assigned before leaving, I knew I had to try it solo. And I jumped at the opportunity to take advantage of a special Indian Airlines "deal" that let you travel anywhere in India for two weeks for $200 as long as you started in New Delhi, didn't return to a previous location, and your final destination was New Delhi. So, I visited the principal Buddhist sites in India. Hard to believe that Gautama Buddha was born in India, yet his birthplace has few Buddhist adherents compared to other countries. One of my districts, Darjeeling, welcomed many Tibetans when they fled from Chinese rule to India. I was able to observe their religion up close. The remote mountainous lands of Tibet and Ladakh captivated me. I really enjoyed the refreshing weather of Kashmir and the Tibetan customs of the Ladakhi peoples. Yet, Afghanistan sounded wild, remote, and off the beaten track! And the lure of seeing a part of the fabled Silk Road and Bamiyan was something I couldn't resist.

But I was anxious and disconcerted. Although it was two years before the Russian invasion, the Hippie Trail was starting to lose its attraction. Few free spirits were still coming out from West Europe and making it to India and Nepal. Even when I visited Goa at the end of my assignment, few Westerners were flocking to the beaches. The idea that I would easily find a woman travel partner on the road and hook up for short time in cities, didn't seem viable. I didn't see any ads posted in Delhi looking for a solo woman traveling companion. It might get very lonely on the road. But I was committed to trying the idea of going solo. My big coup was having a round-the-world Pan Am ticket so at least I could always find my way back home. I just needed to use the ticket wisely. The guides of this Australian overland tour bus were the ones who told me about the Mustafa Hotel in Kabul while we bonded in Jaipur. Your best tips always came from those who had already done the trip! These are the folks who provide those words of wisdom, and caution you about the places to avoid.

I needed to arrange a tour or join one to see Bamiyan, so the Tourist Bureau would play a key role. Since I was just starting my five- to six-month travel, I was worried about running out of money. So once in a town or city, I planned to get around by walking. Walking gives you a feel of a place and you might see an interesting restaurant or hidden park. I knew I needed to head over to a road called Chicken Street which was in an entirely different section of Kabul. I was staying in a hotel whose name I now have forgotten, but it was listed, and one could make a reservation, unlike this Mustafa Hotel. I asked the reception for directions to the Tourist Bureau and they gave me general direction: "Cross the River Kabul and then head…" toward the old city.

Kabul has a semi-arid climate and at 5,900 feet elevation, the weather was temperate in June. It was cooler than Delhi and not humid, which I totally preferred. There wasn't much to see as I strolled along but Kabul is situated in a valley and if you look up and, in the distance, the Hindu Kush mountains were stunningly beautiful surrounding the city. I'm not sure when I sensed that I was being followed. There weren't a lot of people on the street. Once I got closer to the old city, I knew in my gut that a man was following me. I looked around to see if there were any restaurant or tea shop I could whip in and order some food and maybe throw him off-kilter. But I couldn't see any establishment. There started to be some small shops, but I couldn't determine what they sold. I probably was being super sensitive, but this guy had a rifle or some sort of long gun, but then every third Afghan had a gun.

He kept about a block distance behind me. I started to worry. I saw that I was now in a district where all the stores were selling cloth to make the local dress. I was upset and angry that this man continued following me, but I wasn't sure what to do. I peered into a window of a shop and pretended to look at the fabric, but the guy also stopped further back. So, I ducked into the shop where a trio of men were sitting at the counter, drinking tea. I nodded and mumbled, "Salam Alaikum!" Then the door was pushed open and this stalker walked in! Now I was pissed. This was going to stop now and that's when I started yelling. "Why are you following me? I have done nothing wrong! Leave me alone!"

The shop owner immediately sized up the situation, and after a flurry of harsh words, the stalker left. The shop owner saw that I was upset, went to get me a cup of tea, and placed it on a separate table for me with no words. He let me calm down. I asked him if I were close to the Tourist Bureau which I thought was somewhere in the vicinity. The owner knew some English and explained that I was close, just two blocks up and on the right. I never could figure out what the stalker's problem was. At that time, Afghan women attending the university, didn't wear the burqa and, more than likely, wore demure Western clothing. But they always wore a head scarf. I'm not sure what was his intent: to kidnap me, beat me up, threaten me? I had no one to ask.

As I drank my tea and tried to calm down, I thought *This is my first day in Kabul.* If I'm going to be harassed, maybe I needed to quickly revise my planned itinerary. I looked up, smiled at the owner, and said, "Thank you for the tea and your help. I think I'm ready to leave. Can you check the street?" The store owner walked to the door and out on the street. He looked both ways and indicated the coast was clear. I smiled and nodded my head as I left the store. I had clear directions now to the Tourist Bureau. It was only a few blocks away. It seemed safe.

I must say it did throw me off initially. I found the Tourist Office and made arrangements to join a small tour to Bamiyan. And while having chai (tea) at a tea house relaxing, I met a Swede, Carl, who was also exploring the country and looking for a traveling companion. A new opportunity arose on the horizon. I found the Mustafa Hotel and transferred over the next morning to an area in the city that seemed to have more dealings with Westerners. I moved freely around this part of the Old City and never had another instance of a male Afghan stalking me. Carl and I went on the road tour to Bamiyan and Band e Amir Lakes, and I was ecstatic to have seen these places before the Taliban destroyed the standing Buddhas that had been there for centuries. Carl certainly gave me "cover" to continue traveling in Afghanistan. Would I have gone on the trip to Bamiyan alone? Would I have gone earlier to the airlines to depart sooner from Kabul? I'm pretty sure I would have gone to Bamiyan, since that was a long-held dream, but I would have left Kabul immediately after the trip. I probably wouldn't have continued solo to see Tehran, another fundamentalist Muslim capital. To Afghani people, it looked like Carl and I were a couple, together traveling on the road. He made it easier for me to do what I wanted in Afghanistan. *Sometimes, you can't travel solo; you must depend on the kindness of strangers.*

The Legendary Turkana Bus

THERE ARE SOME trips that are engraved on your soul, never to be forgotten! The fabled Turkana Bus is a legend among East African road trips. It was a seven-day adventure expedition through the North West Frontier of Kenya from Nairobi in the south, to the Jade Sea (Lake Turkana) in the north. In 1977 the North West Frontier was a no-man's land. One had to be on the lookout for armed shifta (roaming bands of thieves). There were no "roads" through the frontier, just a worn track laced with huge potholes, scooped out between a seemingly endless high desert environment. If it rained, this track would suddenly become one large mud hole impassable even for a four-wheel-drive vehicle. It didn't rain on my trip. Twelve adventurers signed up for the journey. I was the only "tourist" in the group. The other eleven were an eclectic bunch of diplomats, NGO humanitarian types, and backpackers visiting their relatives in East Africa. Most of them spoke Kiswahili, the lingua franca of East Africa. I could hold my own, since the group was intrigued by my tales from India, having worked on eradicating smallpox, a feat that was thought impossible! I was in Kenya visiting a close friend who was in the same medical school class with me. She was now teaching in the medical school in Nairobi.

After relaxing in Mombasa on the Indian Ocean, camping in Tsavo East with my friends and their nine-month-old son Kevin, climbing Mt. Kenya with Kathy's brother John, they were leaving to go on "Home Leave" to Seattle for two months before returning for another year in Nairobi. Kathy said, "Connie, you can stay in our house for as long as you want, but I think you should check out this trip, *the Turkana Bus,* which goes to a wild, remote area." That's how I heard about it. We would travel in one of these Bedford trucks, that looked like a platform placed on top of a huge cargo truck that stood about 3 ½ feet above the ground. Twenty seats lined the perimeter and faced inward. The back of the truck was stuffed with camping supplies and food. We had a *White* Kenyan Tour Guide/Bwana and Driver rolled into one, and two Kenyan *msaidizi* (assistants). One was another driver, and the other was the cook. This decidedly wasn't your grandmother's Luxury Safari excursion off to see the Big Five wildlife.

Leaving Nairobi, we climbed the escarpment overlooking the Rift Valley and drove to Gil Gil before turning northeast to pass through Nyahururu and Rumuruti before reaching Maralal. From Maralal we continued through Baragoi to South Horr. After a night at South Horr, we continue up through the Chalbi desert to Loiyangalani on the shores of Lake Turkana. Our return route took us back down as far as Baragoi before turning southeast to go through Barsaloi and Wamba on our way to Archers Post and Buffalo Springs game reserve. After two nights in Buffalo Springs/ Samburu, we left the park and drove south to Nairobi, arriving back in town on Friday afternoon.

We had to do only one thing on safari; at each overnight stop, we had to set up the two-man tent that we shared. Depending on your interest (and how soon you wanted to eat dinner), you could "volunteer" to help cook or clean up. Also, if you wanted to have a hot meal at Lake Turkana, you needed to collect firewood, which was placed on the roof of the truck, to carry to the Lake. Seems there were few acacia thorn trees in that area around the inland sea. Otherwise, you could relax in front of the fire, and drink the last cold Tusker beer on that first night. After that, you depended on what alcoholic drink you packed for the trip until you got to the

Lake. This was a young group; I don't think there was anyone over 35 years of age.

Someone in the group was an anthropologist, and he talked a little about the different nomadic groups in the area who lived around Lake Turkana. They included the Turkana, Rendille, Gabbra, Daasanach, Hamar Koke, Karo, Nyagatom, Mursi, Surma, and Molo peoples. Someone else was a bit of a historian and talked about the early colonial explorers and how the lake was first "discovered" by these Austrian explorers and named Lake Rudolph.

On our first night when sufficiently out in the bush, we were visited by roaming bands of Samburu warriors seeking to sell their carved knives, beaded belts, or ostrich-shell necklaces (*which were banned for the tribals searching out the ostrich eggs to use in making necklaces by the government some ten years later*). And yes, I bought one of those necklaces back in the day! On the second day, we had a flat tire! These tires were huge, and it took two to three hours and three men, to change the damn thing. I noticed that we only carried two spares. We were in the middle of nowhere! What could cause a puncture? I would find out soon enough. Whenever we stopped for the night, some nomadic group would find our encampment and show us their wares for sale. The second night, a group of Rendille nomads came and those UN folks who were good Kiswahili speakers were bargaining up a storm. I could only count to ten in Swahili so *kumi* (ten) was my top number. Joe, one of the UN contingent said, "Do you know what they're saying about you, Connie? They say that you're *pretending* to not speak Swahili, but they know you're just being stuck up! But since you're a *Rendille from the "city,"* they can't charge you a high price. And that's why you got that bracelet so cheap!" *I can't believe they really thought I was one of them!* Boy, were they pissed that I got better deals than they, who could speak the language!

The Kenyan cook was excellent, and he had a roaring fire going in no time and was making some delicious Kenya curry with some of the last mangoes and papayas from Nairobi. Then we heard a high-pitched scream coming from my tent, which sent a chill up my back. I ran to the tent, thinking Karen had been bitten by a scorpion or saw a lion on the track. She was crumpled on the ground and holding her foot. "What happened?" I asked. She was still crying with tears pouring down her face.

"I stepped on something," she said.

I went to get a flashlight, as the light was fading fast. Once I could see, I noticed a thick thorn from the acacia tree was stuck up the heel of her foot a good 2 inches! I just touched the 2mm of exposed thorn and she burst out screaming. *There was no way I was going to be able to pull that thing out!* "What can you do, Connie!" she cried. I shook my head and said, "I need to think about this. Let me help you into the tent and then I'll see what's in the first aid kit belonging to the Turkana Bus." I had one of my bad feelings in my gut. I knew what that meant.

So, I went to talk to Bob the guide and his right-hand man. The first aid kit was for minor scrapes. It had some tincture of iodine, Band-Aids, and some salve composed of two antibiotics. I told him the thorn was deeply embedded in the middle of the heel. No way could I pull it out.

"Can you take a knife and cut it out?" asked Bob.

"Are you going to hold her down while I cut 2 inches into the heel with no anesthesia and no antibiotics? Here's what I'm afraid of. If we leave the thorn in, it can fester. I have no idea what dirt and fungus were on the thorn, and, if left in, it could cause septicemia."

"How far are we from the Lake? Is there a clinic or something there?

"There's a police station on the other side of the Lake, and they have a radio that we can use to call the Flying Doctors. It's still one day to the Lake. Or we can turn around and go back to Nairobi, which is a two-day haul." I didn't like either choice.

And then I remembered something I heard while sitting around the campfire on the beach in Mombasa. Someone had been complaining about schools of jellyfish about 1 km down the coast and they were temporarily forbidding swimming. They were talking about the stinger of the jellyfish which was poisonous. And the difficulty of removing it from the arm or leg of someone. An old wives' tale says that villagers would cut papaya, slap it on over the stinger, and leave it for an hour. It seems the papaya has an enzyme, papain, which tenderizes the skin and muscle and makes it easy to remove the stinger. We all laughed! But then later, I remembered my cook in Jaipur, India smashing up papaya and marinating a tough old chicken for about 2 hours before making a curry. It definitely made the tough meat "tender"! I thought, *What's to lose? I might as well try it.*

"Bob, do you have any papaya left on the bus?"

"Let me go ask the cook," and he scurried away. After ten minutes, he came back with a small papaya. "This is the last of the fresh fruit," he said and handed it to me. I jumped up and said, "Thanks." And to myself, I thought *"Here goes nothing."* I went back to my tent where Karen was dosing off. I said, "We were discussing how to get you out and back to Nairobi. In the meantime, I want to try something." I had cut the papaya in half and scraped out the seeds. It was a small papaya and the heel of her foot just fit in the hollow round part. "Do you have a large hiking sock?" She scrounged around and found a dirty sock. Gingerly, I pulled it up around the papaya to hold it close to the foot. "Now we'll wait. Do you have any pain? Here's some Advil. Try to get some sleep. I'll look at the foot in the morning."

I went to wash my hands and then settle down in my sleeping bag. Karen soon drifted off to sleep and so did I. At first light, Karen stirred and asked, "Are you awake, Connie?"

"Yeah, how do you feel?"

"Alright, I'm just worried about my foot."

"Okay, let's look at the foot." I gently pulled off the sock and put the now mushy papaya outside the tent. I sat in front of the door of the tent and unzipped the fly so I could have good light to see and balanced her foot on my thigh. I wiped the remaining papaya away and saw the end of the thorn still sticking out. I pushed down on the heel on either side of the thorn and, to my surprise, the flesh easily pushed down, and the thorn was exposed about an inch and a half. I easily pulled it out of the heel. It was slippery like one had poured oil on it. I held it up in my hand! Karen started to cry and so did I. "Oh my God, it worked!" I said.

The papain tenderized the heel, and I was able to expose more of the thorn and pull it out. The area around the previous embedded thorn looked clean with no signs of infection. I thought we should still soak the foot in iodine. I went running to Bob to say, "The thorn came out, the thorn came out! It's a miracle!" *And this went down in Turkana Bus legend.*

Everyone was counseled to keep wearing their shoes and not to walk barefoot around the tents because acacia thorns were scattered all over. I could only think how close we came to disaster because trying to get her out would have ruined this whole trip! I became famous overnight as being the greatest doctor in the world. She was lucky. It appeared that all the thorn had been removed and she was able to put on a clean sock and walk again, gingerly. The whole camp became enlivened, and we were excited that today, we would see the Jade Sea.

We had been traveling for three days and of course, we lucked out with another flat tire! Once again, people pitched in to help change this huge tire on the truck. I didn't even want to consider what we would do if we got a third flat! Once we would get to Loiyangalani, there was a gas station and they could fix the tires, but we needed to get there. Now, all we had seen for 3 days in this semi-arid desert was the occasional acacia tree and you couldn't imagine that there would be a lake somewhere in the midst of this. How is that possible? Then the truck started climbing up a steep incline and at the top of the ridge, Bob stopped the Bedford! And lo and behold, stretched out in front of us was a brilliant huge Jade Sea! We all grabbed our cameras and sprinted outside. They hadn't been kidding us; there was an honest to goodness lake ahead. And with the temperature for the last few days at 40+celsius (104 F), all anyone could think about was jumping in Lake Turkana! *There was just one slight problem: Nile crocodiles!* The lake was full of crocodiles!

So, this is the legendary Jade Sea! Lake Turkana, formerly known as Lake Rudolf, the world's largest permanent, freshwater desert lake. Located in northern Kenya, its far northern end crosses into Ethiopia. It's also the world's largest alkaline lake. By volume, it is the world's fourth largest salt lake after the Caspian Sea, Issyk-Kul in Kyrgyzstan, and Lake Van in Turkey, and among all lakes, it ranks 24th.

Although the lake commonly has been, and to some degree still is, used for drinking water, its salinity (slightly brackish) and very high levels of fluoride (much higher than in fluoridated water) generally make it unsuitable for drinking. However, for the various nomadic tribes that live around its shore and for their livestock, it's been their source of drinking water for centuries. And it's also been a source of diseases spread by contaminated water. Increasingly, the communities on the lake's shores have to rely on underground springs for drinking water. The same characteristics that make it unsuitable for drinking also limit its use in irrigation. The climate was hot and very dry.

At some unknown time, the lake acquired the name, the Jade Sea, from its turquoise color seen approaching from a distance. The color comes from algae that rise to the surface in calm weather. And if you look at satellite pictures of the area, it shows up as a brilliant Jade color! Mankind just can't leave well enough alone. Lake Turkana is now threatened by the construction of Gilgel Gibe III Dam in Ethiopia (2020) due to the damming of the Omo river which supplies most of the lake's water. The communities tried to fight the construction of the dam, and whoever was responsible for the Environmental Study appears to have brushed aside the importance of 300,000 people who use the lake as a source of water. Also, the report stating the dam was being built in an earthquake area didn't seem to be a deterrent until it is! When I was the Regional

Infectious Disease Advisor at USAID/Nairobi, I tried to interest the USAID Kenyan Environmental program to evaluate the relationship of the Lake to the nomadic peoples that depended on that resource.

But back in 1977, all we could think about was jumping in the cool waters (maybe not so cool), and relaxing and finding a bar with some very cold Tusker beer! Oh yeah, there was another small problem: the Nile crocodile.

The Nile crocodile (Crocodylus niloticus) is a native to freshwater habitats in Africa, where it is present in 26 countries. Due to its widespread occurrence and stable population trend, *it isn't endangered!* (So, I don't regret getting a briefcase made of the crocodile skin in Senegal). It's widely distributed throughout sub-Saharan Africa, occurring mostly in the central, eastern, and southern regions of the continent. It lives in different types of aquatic environments such as lakes, rivers, swamps, and marshlands. Although capable of living in saline environments, this species is rarely found in saltwater, but occasionally inhabits deltas and brackish lakes. Lake Turkana is brackish. On average, the adult male Nile crocodile is between 3.5 and 5 m (11.5 and 16.4 ft) in length and weighs 225 to 750 kg (500 to 1,650 lbs.). I think I can say that you really don't want to encounter a crocodile in the water! It's the largest freshwater predator in Africa. They have thick, scaly, heavily armored skin.

Nile crocodiles are opportunistic *alpha predators*; a very aggressive species of crocodile, they're capable of taking almost any animal within their range. They're *generalists*, taking a variety of prey (especially human). Their diet consists mostly of different species of fish, reptiles, birds, and mammals. They ambush their prey and can wait for hours, days, and even weeks for the suitable moment to attack. They're agile and wait for the opportunity for a prey to come well within attack range. Even swift prey aren't immune to attack. Like other crocodiles, the Nile crocodile has an extremely powerful bite that is unique among all animals, and sharp, conical teeth that sink into flesh, allowing for a grip that's almost impossible to loosen. They can apply high levels of force an extended time, a great advantage for holding down large prey underwater to drown.

Nairobi has some great bookstores, but I only came across the beautiful tabletop photo book, *Eyelids of Morning* by Peter Beard after I returned from Lake Turkana! It recounted anything and everything about the Lake Turkana crocodiles. The book only confirmed my intuition about not swimming there. However, my fellow travel mates couldn't wait to get in the water. *I told them that crocodiles preferred white meat, but they didn't believe me.* I volunteered instead, to look out for crocodiles on land while lying under the shade of a palm tree. Our guide had noted that this particular inlet didn't *normally* have a lot of crocodiles. Some of our group wanted to find the El Molo community, who lived in the southeastern part of the Lake. So, they went out on flimsy reed boats to go fishing. I also declined the ride on the reed boat. Now for me, what I considered risky was swimming in the Jade Sea and rafting on a thin reed boat. Different strokes for different folks!

All's well that ends well. We only stayed at the Lake for a day and a half before heading back. And yes, it earned its name as *"the toughest bus ride in the world."* It could have ended up as the worst trip in the world if I hadn't removed that thorn out of my tent mate's foot. *It did make a great tale!*

Traveling in Yemen- Carefully

SOME COUNTRIES WERE easy to travel in. Yemen wasn't one of those!

Situated in a mountain valley at an altitude of 2,200 m (7,217 ft), the Old City of Sana'a is defined by an extraordinary density of rammed earth and burnt brick towers rising several stories above stone-built ground floors, strikingly decorated with geometric patterns of fired bricks and white gypsum. The ochre of the buildings, blends into the bistre-colored earth of the nearby mountains. Within the city, minarets pierce the skyline and spacious green bustans (gardens) are scattered between the densely packed houses, mosques, hammams (Islamic bathhouses), and caravanserais.

Yemen has long existed at the crossroads of cultures with a strategic location in terms of trade on the west of the Arabian Peninsula. It had a long turbulent history even before North and South Yemen were united in 1990. The country was divided between the dueling Ottoman and British empires in the early twentieth century. The Zaydi Mutawakkilite Kingdom of Yemen (North Yemen) was established after World War I in the northwestern part of Yemen before it became the Yemen Arab Republic in 1962. South Yemen remained a British protectorate known as the Aden Protectorate until 1967 when it first became an independent state and later, a Marxist-Leninist state. The two Yemeni states united to form the modern Republic of Yemen in 1990.

There was a short period after the creation of the Republic but before the country degenerated into outright war, that held a certain fascination for diplomats, backpackers, and lovers of the exotic! Yemen was known for its fabled capital of Old Sana'a with its famous gingerbread-colored Tower Houses declared a World Heritage site. In December 1992, I was working in Addis Ababa, Ethiopia in the WHO Emergency Preparedness and Response Center on infectious diseases. Some eighteen months earlier, I was caught up in a swiftly moving civil war, when the Tigrayan rebel army stormed into the capital, defeating the Russian-backed Ethiopian government forces. The capital had almost settled back to normal under a Provisional government. I got an email from two friends who worked with me in my former posting in Dakar, Senegal asking if I could be enticed to do a trip to Yemen. They proposed first a visit to Addis and then a week-long trip to the newly created Republic of Yemen.

I hadn't seen Fabienne and Kristin since I left for an assignment in Ethiopia. Both were soon to be departing from Senegal to their next postings and they were up for an adventure before being scattered to the four corners of the world. Fabienne worked for the Swiss Embassy in Nairobi but we had met long before in Abidjan in a jogging club called the Hash House Harriers. The other friend was Kristin who was a junior diplomat in the Norwegian Embassy in Dakar. She had been adopted in Ethiopia as an infant by Norwegian parents and raised in Norway and eventually entered the Diplomatic Corps. They both were excited to meet my daughter Romene whom I adopted during the civil war in Addis Ababa. You can read about that adventure in my memoir *Three Years in Ethiopia, How a Civil War and Epidemics Led Me to My Daughter.* How could I pass up this adventure with my friends?

I looked up the Republic of Yemen to find out more about it before my friends arrived. The first thing you should know about Yemen is that there are three main ethnic groups in the country: the mountain people (they live in North Yemen), the coastal people (they live in the South and West Yemen), and the Bedouins. These three groups differ in their cultural characteristics, customs, and traditions. We only had time to head north out of Sana'a, so we were going to be immersed in the mountain people's culture and dress.

Yemeni claimed that they, not the Ethiopians first discovered coffee! (*Tell that to the Ethiopians!*) The northern highlands in former North Yemen were famous for their villages and fortress Tower Houses. And they were proud of their traditional Yemeni dress. Yemeni men wore a distinctive long robe or a striped skirt (futa) with a curved dagger (jambiyya) at the front, attached to a decorative belt. Yemen is also known for qhat, it's most popular plant, with effects similar to amphetamine. It's the main social activity in the afternoon, but I'll get to that later.

In our entire trip to the north, every male national I saw was dressed in the traditional Yemeni attire: thoobs and futa skirts. Thoob (also called "thawb" or "thobe") is a loose ankle-length garment with long sleeves. Such robe-like garments are common among Arab countries, and Yemen is no exception. Men in Yemen also notably sport distinctive headgear. There were plenty of different headdresses used in this country. The most popular and widespread was the turban and the alqaweq. Headdresses in Yemen are very important accessories. In the past, there were even class distinctions by the type of headgear. Today, no such divides exist, but usually, you can tell a lot by the headdress of a person!

Yemeni women usually wear very colorful outfits, with a lot of embroideries, jewelry, and decorative elements. This is in sharp contrast to the dark clothing usually seen in other Muslim countries. Yemeni women cover their heads as a sign of modesty. Those who live in urban areas wear veils and scarves daily while women from rural areas sometimes forgo covering their heads.

In 1992, there were the occasional reports of kidnapping of foreigners, but they were usually ransomed easily. The new government wanted to emphasize prioritizing tourism. You could get a tourist visa on entry and my friends had already contacted a tour agency for a car and driver to head north. The tour agency was responsible for getting permits to travel outside of the capital. There were government checkpoints at strategic crossroads, and things were considered fairly safe during the period we traveled to Yemen. My intuition told me now was the time to go. It was a short flight from Addis Ababa, Christmas was already celebrated, and this was the perfect ending to the year: an all-girls trip!

The airport in Sana'a was fairly small and not bustling like in Nairobi. Welcome to Sana'a! We had booked a hotel in one of the Tower Houses in the Old City. It took us less than 10 minutes to get through immigration and we were out. ***Dorothy, we're not in Kansas anymore;*** we're in the Middle East. It looked different, felt different, and was different. The taxis dropped us off at the converted Tower House hotel smack dab in the middle of the Old City. Everyone wore the national dress. I don't remember a lot of women in the streets, but they were present. At the reception desk, they said we were on the sixth floor and we would get help carrying our suitcases up the stairs. No elevator! And the steps were immense! It seemed like the step risers were 25 inches high. Just walking up and down the steps would provide plenty of exercise. On our floor, there was a *mufrage* (sitting room) with oriental carpets and lounging pillows on the floor, for socializing, and then two bedrooms off it. There was also a bathroom that had a primitive shower and a toilet. We arranged our things hastily in the bedrooms and then ran up to the roof, which was open on four sides. You had a bird's eye view of the city! My friends had booked us for 2 nights in Sana'a, and then we would go upcountry for three nights and return for one last night in Sana'a before heading back to Addis Ababa.

We had not planned a tour of Sana'a. We just wanted to wander the narrow alleyways and head for the souk to pick up some dried and fresh fruit and nuts. We wandered the narrow warren of streets and strolled into shops to admire the handicrafts. It was going to be hard deciding what to select to take back home. I saw some old silver jewelry to die for. But then the curved knives that the men wore were outstanding. This was going to be difficult.

Yemenite silversmithing refers to the work of Jewish silversmiths from Yemen. They were highly acclaimed craftsmen who dominated craft production in precious metals in the southern Arabian Peninsula from the 18th through the mid-20th century, a period and region during which Muslims didn't engage in this work.

Between June 1949 and September 1950, almost the entire Jewish community in Yemen, including nearly every silversmith in the country, immigrated to Israel in an airborne mass migration known as Operation Magic Carpet. Muslims appear to have entered silversmithing in Yemen in the mid-1950s as the Jews departed for Israel. Mass-produced gold and silver jewelry began to be imported into Yemen in the 1930s and dominated the market by the end of the 20th century, causing traditional silversmithing to dwindle. Of course, silversmithing in Israel probably improved immensely!

According to Mark. S. Wagner, Professor of Arabic literature and Islamic law at Louisiana State University, it is difficult to say how silver- and gold-smithing came to be regarded as occupations that were too impure for Muslims in Yemen to engage in. Jewish silversmiths in this region, however, sometimes moonlighted as dentists, since their jeweler's pliers could be used to draw teeth. Notwithstanding, before their departure, it was generally accepted in Yemen that specialist silversmiths enjoyed an influential status that towered over all others within the Jewish community, since silversmiths belonged to the community's spiritual elite.

Melted silver coins produced jambiyya (dagger) hilts, bridal jewelry, and other silver objects. The Maria Theresa thaler, a trade coin that was minted continuously since 1741, was especially favored for its consistent silver content and fineness (containing an 83% silver content; the rest an alloy). The thaler currency was widely used in the Arabian Peninsula and especially in Yemen owing to the Mocha coffee trade with the French, and a Yemeni request that coffee be paid with thalers.

When you walk through the gate of Bab al-Yemen, you know you're in another time and place. You're transported back to the medieval period. Shopping made us ravenous. We found a restaurant serving Yemeni food and sat down to order. We were the only women in the restaurant. We got a lot of stares but no harassment, and the food came quickly. We ordered the national dish which is a sort of stew and they make this delicious bread, which is like naan flatbread. The Yemeni main meal is at lunchtime and afterwards, they like to relax. So, we hurried back to our hotel to order Yemeni tea and collapse in our mufrage room. It was perfect for napping and reading whatever book we had brought along. Sometime later, Muhammed, our driver, security, and all-around guide, dropped in to update us when we would leave in the morning. It would be good to get out of the capital to see the "real Yemen."

We would travel north tomorrow headed for Dar al-Hajar, a stone castle rising in the West and on to one of the most remote cities in Yemen, Shaharah.

It was exciting to finally be on the road in our white SUV. The fascinating part of the trip would be the landscape, a high semi-arid place of fantastic mountain ridges and shapes. Every major juncture had a Police roadblock. Mohammed would hand over the travel permits, and they would read them and then look into the vehicle. Soldiers were amused to see three ladies in the back. Around about ten every morning, Mohammed said, "I need to stop by the market." We would wait in the car while he was gone for about twenty minutes. He always came back with a huge bag of a type of green herb.

"What is that?" we asked.

"It's qhat."

We had heard about qhat. It was some type of narcotic, a mild stimulant. When we stopped for lunch the first day out, we discussed among ourselves whether our driver should be consuming qhat and driving at the same time? I said, "I think we don't have much choice. This is a cultural thing!"

We were headed for Dar al-Hajar, popularly called the "Stone House" or "Rock Palace." It was a former royal palace located in

Wadi Dhar about 15 kilometers (9.3 mi) from Sana'a, Yemen. Built in the 1920s as the summer retreat of Yahya Muhammad Hamid ed-Din, ruler of Yemen from 1904 to 1948, it sits on top of a structure built even earlier in 1786 for the scholar al-Imam Mansour. The palace remained in the royal family until the Yemen revolution of 1962. When you first come around a bend and see the Rock Palace, it looks like an enchanting, otherworldly structure seemingly growing out of a rock cliff! The palace was something unique that I had not seen before. When we were in Yemen (1992), people couldn't go inside. Or at least, we couldn't go inside. It was still stunning just to get out and take photos of the house. The palace was now a museum.

I'm not sure where we stayed the first night out, but it was a tower house and we were the only people in it! We climbed up the stairs to the mesfrage floor and found where the bedrooms were. Soon hot black tea was brought up to the sitting rooms. And we relaxed. Mohammed had his bag of qhat, so he was relaxed. He stayed with us until the food arrived. Two men carried in an array of Yemeni food which were mostly what I take as curries. And their delicious bread! I thought for sure we would meet some women, at least the ones who would bring us food. But alas, that was not to be. Probably, since most of the other guests to this house would have been male nationals, the women would cook, and the servers would be male relatives. We fell off to sleep quite early.

I don't remember hearing any muezzin calls during the night. Now I was dead tired, but I'm wondering if they practice an "Islam lite" program in the North. Anyway, a breakfast of bread and tea was served around 8 am. Fabienne and Kirstin also reported that they slept the sleep of the dead. But we were rearing to take off for the remote village of Shaharah. The dirt roads got smaller and closer to the side of the cliff that dropped miles into a valley below. I was thinking, *I'm glad I don't have to drive this road.*

Shaharah is certainly not the only fortified mountain village in Yemen, but it's definitely among the most spectacular. At 2,600 m (8,530 ft) above sea level in the middle of a craggy mountain landscape of fissures and gorges, the town's landscape is infused in drama. Originally, the only approach to the village was via an impressive, arched stone bridge, which spans one of the mountain gorges. Now, there's a death-defying road that leads to the village. Right before you can take this road was a wide parking area that had about six SUV type vehicles and 20 tribal men lounging around. They checked our travel permits and we would be escorted up to the village by one of the jeeps! So, six turban-covered tribals jumped in the back of the SUV-vehicle each with their Kalashnikov rifles. This was a one-way track only; just wide enough for one vehicle to use the path.

We followed our "escort" directly into the village and Mohammed drove to our Tower House where we unloaded our gear. It was about noon, still too early to eat. We had hot tea and then we felt like exploring. Muhammed came back with our male "chaperone." He was from the village and would guide and escort us all over so we wouldn't have any problems. He didn't know any English, so the guiding part lacked a little history. But he knew what the tourists wanted to see and first we wanted to visit the famous Bridge of Shaharah. Our guide had his trusty Kalashnikov rifle and bandolier of bullets to protect us!

The village's secluded position and its sole point of entry made Shaharah incredibly inaccessible. Water cisterns within the village and nearby terraced fields would enable the village to endure even lengthy sieges. For centuries, the village successfully withstood innumerable armies and conquerors. In fact, it wasn't until the use of air force during the 1960s, in the first of many Yemeni Civil Wars, that the village's isolated location was finally shattered.

Shahareh, Shehara, or Shaharah (whatever…) is a large mountain village and capital of Shaharah District of the 'Amran Governorate, Yemen. The village overlooks undulating waves of mountains to the south and shimmering hot plains to the north. The village, which lies on top of a sharp mountain of the same name, Jabal Shaharah, consists of several old stone tower houses and a cistern. But the area is noted for its limestone arch footbridge, constructed in the 16th century by a local lord to connect two villages across a deep gorge.

Today's bridge was built in the 16th century. However, the remains of at least two earlier bridges can still be detected. The bottom of the former bridges is located at a lower level. Traces of a pathway that led at some stage to those lower bridges were still visible. The 100-m deep gorge that could only be crossed by the bridge, itself protected by a solid gate, was the second line of defense against potential intruders from the valley. Note that anyone trying to cross the bridge could easily be shot at from the stairs leading upwards to the village!

Since the 9th century, the village also held a reputation of being an important place of Islamic learning, and scholars throughout the region were well known in the town. Unfortunately, the village now is in Northern Yemen, where the Shia Insurgency has turned the region into a de facto war zone. Not sure if you can even visit the village today (2020). *The bridge didn't disappoint!* I wondered how men constructed the bridge given their limited knowledge of physics. It brought back my thoughts to the famous film, *The Bridge Over the River Kwai* set in Burma during WWII.

We didn't test the durability of the bridge but only marveled at its beauty and dramatic exposure, seeming to dangle thousands of meters above the gorge. With one last look at the bridge, we headed back to lodgings and looked forward to the evening because Mohammed was going to teach us how to chew qhat! We ordered a big meal because this wasn't the time to be hypoglycemic. And we just laid back. Soon after eating, Muhammed showed up and held up the bag, saying, "Personally selected by your driver with all the best leaves." And we were slowly mesmerized by his voice.

If there's one word that I heard more than any other during my stay in Yemen, it was the word "qhat." And the reason that word is so important is that, at approximately 2 pm every single day, the entire nation seemed to stop whatever they were doing and focused on qhat. We could note it in the capital when people disappeared off the streets.

Qhat is a plant that's grown all over Yemen on what seems to be every square inch of land, whether in the valleys or on the mountainsides, that could be used to grow a plant. When the leaves of the plant are fresh, they are chewed, an activity that leads to a state of increased excitement with the possibility of mild euphoria as a bonus. This state is the result of a stimulant similar to amphetamine that's found in the plant and which, using the best description I've heard, acts as if you're drinking endless cups of very strong coffee. Qhat, and the substance it contains, is illegal in many Western countries and its consistent use is mostly limited to Yemen, Somalia, Ethiopia, Djibouti, and a handful of other countries in the same geographical area. It's also legal in those countries.

In Yemen, people chew qhat while walking, sitting, talking, driving, working, and just about anything else they might be doing. And when I say "people," I'm referring to what appears to be the entire over-18 male population of the country. Supposedly, women also chew the leaves, but I surmise someone has to cook the midday meal and look after the children. I saw many a gathering of men chewing this plant, but I never saw any women outside the house chewing! But then our little group traveled upcountry and never met any woman! Still, on our entire trip, I found it strange that we were never invited into a house to talk to any of the women.

It's quite traditional for Yemeni males to wear a jambiya every day, a curved ceremonial blade that's displayed in the front by wedging it into a thick belt. And when qhat time comes around, most males suddenly have a huge bag of leaves hanging from the handle of their knife so that they have easy access to their qhat.

This isn't just some occasional hobby. Every male I observed suggested by their actions, that they were addicted to qhat. I supposed that the only way they could stop chewing it was if they had no money at all and couldn't afford even the cheapest variety, which cost about 500 rials (USD 2) for a huge bag. *Did I try it? Come on!* We were curious, and we decided that on our last day in the north in the remote village of Shaharah we would ask Muhammad to introduce us to the world of qhat. We would try it once, in the presence of someone we trusted, and he could purchase it, so we had a good selection.

So, how does chewing qhat work? First thing in the morning, go to the qhat Market to buy your daily supply, choosing the best quality that you can afford. Qhat typically stays fresh for one day, so most people buy a new batch every day.

After lunch, around 2:00 pm, pull out your bag of qhat, find a comfortable mufrage (a sitting room designed specifically for chewing qhat) that can be found in every home, restaurant, and hotel and may sometimes be located outside) and get into the proper qhat chewing position (sitting on the floor, relaxed, leaning on a cushion).

Mufrage Somewhere in Yemen

3:01 pm – Start chewing qhat by first pulling the leaves out of the plastic bag. Then, place a few leaves and stems into your mouth and chew on them for a minute before stuffing those leaves and stems, using your tongue, into the inner cheek on one side of your mouth. Continue chewing the leaves slowly, squeezing out the juice, while stuffing more and more leaves into your mouth the entire time until you have a bulge in your cheek the size of a watermelon. Stuff, chew, repeat. You repeat the process, never spitting the growing mass of leaves out of your mouth.

I guarantee you that your jaw will get tired. 4:00 pm – Keep on chewing qhat, crunching up those leaves and growing that bulge.

5:00 pm – Don't stop now! Keep chewing.

Okay, my little circle of friends was fed up after one hour! My jaw ached. We couldn't go on! Once we had a thick mass of broken leaves mashed into a mushy ball, we started wondering how to make these leaves just disappear! I was looking for a discreet place to spit out my wad in the living room! (Obviously, not on the carpet). Yeah, there are the hardy and fierce who can chew till the cows go home. But our little band was ready to give up the ghost.

Sometime in the early evening, the qhat session finally ends, and you spit out the remaining qhat from your mouth. You drink a cup of black tea and then you sit there on the cushioned floor of the mufrage, trying to engage in some conversation with the others around you until it's time for sleep.

What are the effects of qhat?

As mentioned above, qhat users get a bit excited and as a result, they will often become extremely talkative and hyper, spitting out words in a rapid and animated fashion to anyone who will listen. However, it also seemed to me that just as many users I saw were perfectly content to sit in silence, staring at the wall and minding their own business.

Behind the scenes, your blood pressure and heart rate increase, you lose your appetite, and to top it off, you become constipated. Long term effects may include cancer of the mouth, depression, and psychosis, all fun stuff.

So, my experience chewing qhat in Yemen? It was okay. Just... *Seemed like quite an effort for such a little buzz.* The qhat made me a bit spacey and somewhat hyper, and I had a good time as a result, but it took four hours of chewing leaves to get there. However, with a 65% unemployment rate in Yemen, I can understand the appeal. But for me, all that chewing was a painstaking process as the inside of my mouth became sore and raw and the stuff initially kept me awake at night.

Would I do it again? Sure, simply because that's the thing to do in Yemen, and in the end, it was a social activity. Had I not chewed qhat, I probably would have regretted missing the experience. Personally, I prefer a couple of tokes from a joint with Acapulco Gold, because that's a lot quicker and you get higher! *It was the experience, dude!*

Since 2011, Yemen has been in a state of the political crisis starting with street protests against poverty, unemployment, corruption, and president Saleh's plan to amend Yemen's constitution and eliminate the presidential term limit, in effect making him president for life. A lot of people didn't like that idea. The conflict had its roots in the failure of a political transition supposed to bring stability to Yemen following an Arab Spring uprising that forced its longtime authoritarian president, Ali Abdullah Saleh, to hand over power to his deputy, Abdrabbuh Mansour Hadi, in 2011. As president, Mr. Hadi struggled to deal with a variety of problems, including attacks by jihadists, a separatist movement in the south, the continuing loyalty of security personnel to Saleh, as well as corruption, unemployment, and food insecurity.

The Houthi movement (known formally as Ansar Allah), which champions Yemen's Zaidi Shia Muslim minority and fought a series of rebellions against Saleh during the previous decade, took advantage of the new president's weakness by taking control of their northern heartland of Saada province and neighboring areas.

Disillusioned with the transition, many ordinary Yemenis, including Sunnis, supported the Houthis, and in late 2014 and early 2015 the rebels gradually took over the capital Sana'a. The Houthis and security forces loyal to Saleh, who was thought to have backed his erstwhile enemies in a bid to regain power, then attempted to take control of the entire country, forcing Mr. Hadi to flee abroad in March 2015.

Alarmed by the rise of a group they believed to be backed militarily by the regional Shia power Iran, A Saudi-led multinational coalition intervened in the conflict in Yemen in March 2015. Saudi Arabia and eight other mostly Sunni Arab states began an air campaign aimed at defeating the Houthis, ending Iranian influence in Yemen and restoring Mr. Hadi's government. The coalition received logistical and intelligence support from the United States, UK, and France.

What's happened since then? All Hell broke out! In my mind, this is really the continuation of the long and painful struggle between the two giant schisms in Islam that keep killing each other until, in the end, both will become irrelevant. At the start of the war, Saudi officials forecasted that it would last only a few weeks. But four years of military stalemate have followed. Not to mention the immense humanitarian crisis.

Coalition ground troops landed in the southern port city of Aden in August 2015 and helped drive the Houthis and their allies out of much of the south over the next few months. Well, this war wasn't going to end anytime soon. *I look at the destruction and destitution of Yemen and I remember with fondness the hospitality and the Tower Houses in North Yemen. In our minds, the risk was worth it in 1992.*

BE OPEN TO NEW FRIENDS- IT CAN LEAD TO NOVEL ADVENTURES

One of the eleven things I learned from Smallpox Field Work was: *being friendly and open to new people in unlikely places can lead to new adventures.* It can be difficult to be the first person to approach someone and to introduce yourself. It's especially stressful if one is traveling solo. I know the hype that it's empowering and life-changing to travel solo, particularly for women travelers. And yes, it can be empowering, but taking that first step and risking possible rejection isn't easy. Let's be clear about that.

Certainly, in the early years, I was usually traveling with a group. For example, my Girl Scout (GS) troop was chosen to go to the Girl Scout Senior Roundup in Button Bay Vermont, in July 1962, where 9,000 Girl Scouts gathered from around the nation. In each GS Council, only a limited number of troops could go. You were selected on merit, and our troop from Mt Diablo GS council was selected. We left on the train from Oakland and transferred back east, to another train to go up to Maine. I remember being so proud of our troop being selected to go. And the people we met. Our troop from Concord CA was an outdoors troop. We had hiked in numerous National Forests and Yosemite. I *remember dreaming maybe one day I could trek to the basecamp of Mt Everest!* Participating in this national and international Roundup helped me gain confidence in my abilities.

The next major decision that I faced was where to go to University. My older brother went to Gonzaga University in Spokane Washington. Selecting a college wasn't the gut-wrenching decision it is today. You looked up a couple of colleges and selected one to apply to. I just wanted to go away to University, to test my wings and to meet individuals who weren't Californians. My older brother headed up to Gonzaga and said he liked the college, so I thought to apply to the same one. Then GU started a new program, Gonzaga in Florence, which invited juniors to study in Europe. Colbert headed off his sophomore year to Florence since pre-med students had too many critical science courses in junior year. And that's how I left for Spokane for my freshman year all alone without my brother to shepherd me through the process. And it's probably good that I braved the train trip alone, seeing that I met fellow Gonzagans and other college students going up to school. And that was the start of my travel bug!

I started this section about being open to meeting new people. I think you would also agree with me on just how valuable travel is. As you read the following four chapters, you'll concur that travel doesn't just open the door to opportunities you would never experience at home. It helps you meet new people, who often share a different perspective on life.

My First Octoberfest

YOU CAN READ about Octoberfest and now view countless YouTube videos of college students drinking their way through Europe. But in 1964, I wasn't sure exactly what it would be like. I touched on Octoberfest in an earlier chapter about the Florence year. Before letting the group of students take off into the festival grounds, we got some cautionary words from our chaperone, Father Reginald, the director for our GIF group. We should go in small groups and visit the various tents. Most of us weren't used to drinking (*and some of us weren't of the drinking age by U.S. standards, so beware of the effects of alcohol*). The Germans weren't going to ask for IDs, so relax. However, the bus would depart promptly at 11:15 pm. Our hotel was in some little town about 40 minutes away. So, if we wanted to sleep tonight, don't be late for the bus! It waits for no man.

I was in a group of three and I was the youngest in our whole Gonzaga in Florence (GIF) group. My parents weren't drinkers and only on Thanksgiving Day or Christmas would you normally find us sharing some wine with dinner in California. This was the Davis house pre-Florence. But once Colbert got back from his year in Florence, he started introducing the family to various wines, particularly from Europe. But I started on my sophomore trip to Florence before I could gain his insight.

I thought Europe was so different and impressive as compared to the states. The architecture was centuries older than anything we erected in America. The German people looked so homogeneous: all

91

tall and blond. Yet the festival drew people from all over Europe, so there was a polyglot of languages. I don't remember seeing another African American woman on my entire orientation trip through Europe to Italy. I never thought about the diversity of the USA before this tour but was immediately struck how *homogeneous* each of the European cities was. Germans looked and spoke a different language from the Dutch and the Italians, yet in their countries, they were the same. And I suppose, because I was so different from my fellow students, I stood out as being distinct and striking.

There appeared to be a myriad of huge white tents and depending on the traditional songs being played, there was a distinct ambiance in each tent. It seemed that each of the 50+ round tables held twenty riotous men swinging these huge German steins of beer! *A stein holds 34 fl oz or 1 liter!* Now the problem with German beer is that the alcohol content is higher than what's in a U.S. beer. And, you also have to eventually find a place to pee! And that can be a problem, even for the camel (me). I never bought one beer during the whole night. The Germans also supplied me with free food to eat. One tent had a decidedly younger college crowd. One table made space for our group and I sat down next to Hans who was a university student in Munich. He was studying languages and was really good in English. We hit it off and he asked, "Do you want to get away from the noise and walk around a bit?"

I said, "I'd love to, but I need to keep an eye on the time, and I'm not sure I should go alone with you without my friends."

Hans replied, "Where do you have to be?"

"I've got to be in the parking lot to find the big bus at 10:50 pm!"

"I promise, I will get you there before time!" And we took off.

There was a section of the fairgrounds that had rides and funky sites where you throw balls at objects to see if you can win a prize. But there was a huge Ferris Wheel in the center. We got in line for the Ferris wheel! Now when was the last time you experienced something for the very first time? Do you remember the first time you went up in a Ferris wheel? For me, I think I was nine years old and still in Chicago and at some State Fair. So, it was almost like experiencing something for the very first time, certainly in Germany! It was a towering Ferris wheel and at the top, you had a magical view of the city. It looked like a fairytale land stretched out before you with twinkling lights. And there's nothing like a kiss at the top of the turn of the Ferris Wheel as you hang suspended for that second in time! I knew I would never see Hans again, but it felt so exciting and thrilling. And when the ride was over, he walked me slowly to the bus in the parking lot. Some of my classmates were already on the coach and fast asleep. We just hugged each other, and I hauled myself up on the bus and turned around to wave one last time. *A perfect Octoberfest!*

Speed Climbing Mt. Kenya

❦

OKAY, I WOULD be lying if I told you I wasn't disappointed (I was pissed) that I couldn't climb Mt. Kilimanjaro, which straddled the border between Kenya and Uganda. You might remember that I climbed to the base camp of Mt. Everest in Nepal when I took a much-deserved vacation from tracking down smallpox cases in India (1976). That climb is well detailed in my book, **Searching for Sitala Mata:** *Eradicating Smallpox in India.* After the celebrations in India when the Global Certification Team did certify India smallpox free, I decided to climb Kilimanjaro when I went to visit my medical school friends who were then teaching in the medical school in Kenya. I wrote to them asking if they knew how to contact a trekking team that wouldn't mind taking on an additional solo client. They promised to ferret out the information and get me signed up.

So, I was looking forward to putting the highest mountain in Africa under my belt of accomplishments. Imagine my disappointment when I finally got to Kenya to find out the dream was an illusion. Turns out Kathy and Bob had to rescind their offer to lend me their Toyota Landcruiser to drive to Uganda. The *perfect* East African Union between Kenya, Uganda, and Tanzania was having a very acrimonious divorce and if the jeep crossed over the border, it wouldn't be allowed to reenter. But they worked to convince me that what I really wanted to do was to climb to Mt. Kenya with Kathy's brother John instead! First, it would be cheaper, since I was already in Kenya, and the climb would only be three days. Kili takes two weeks and, ultimately, many people don't reach the top due to altitude sickness. Because Mt. Kenya is so quick, even if you start to have high altitude sickness, you're heading down anyway on the third day. *You can't fight destiny!* I had a climbing partner right here in Kenya, so I started researching the details of the climb.

Just as in Nepal, there are Kenyan porters who specialize in carrying your pack and setting up camp and cooking for you. Mt. Kenya is 17,057 ft altitude and although it's easier than Kilimanjaro, it was still a challenge. My friends were preparing their home leave travel and John would be going back with them, so we needed to do this climb soon for John to be back in time for the departure. That didn't give me much time to prepare myself psychologically.

We still needed to drive to Mt. Kenya and Kathy had more faith in me learning to handle their Landcruiser over Kenyan roads, since I had a Toyota Landcruiser in India! She didn't want her brother messing up the SUV gears, so they planned to take the whole family to Samburu park, far away from the tourist haunts. We would practice fording streams and making sure I didn't stall the jeep mid-stream in a river. You had to make sure that the water didn't go above a certain level (something about the carburetor.) I practiced taking the vehicle slow and steady through the various rivers. The first time was truly scary, and I actually went too fast, but all's well that ends well. *There was just one warning that they gave me: under no circumstances was I to use the winch that was located on the front of the jeep.* They were having trouble with the mechanism and repairing it would cost more than they wanted to outlay at that time, so please do not operate the winch!

"Why would I want to operate the winch?" I asked. "I don't plan on going over a cliff and having to haul the Landcruiser up!" *Besides, I thought, I'm not good with mechanical things. I was glad John was on this trip because if we needed to change a tire, he would come in handy.* So, we ran around getting food for the trip, packing it in containers, and weighing the packs. And we were off! The road to

Mt Kenya from Nairobi takes about five hours. It's the kind of road that a Landcruiser is built for. Not too many deep potholes. Kathy had already called ahead and organized the porters. We just needed to check in at the porter station and give our names. John and I got to know one another. Of course, there was the usual sibling rivalry.

"Actually, I'm glad Kathy insisted that you drive. She's always bad mouthing me about how I drive, and I don't want to mess up her car. Now you, Davis, can do no wrong, so even if you crash the car, it won't be a problem!"

"Thanks for your vote of confidence," I said. "Wiley and I go back to those first days at UCSF School of Medicine. We women were outnumbered. Kathy, Betty, and I formed a clique." Betty was the other freshman med student who lived in my house off Parnassus. We shared this wonderful huge gingerbread house with two senior women med students who were mostly on the wards and we rarely saw them unless they were doing night duty and home during the day. They were anxious about where they would get in for internship and residency. Wiley lived over on the other side near San Francisco General in the Mission District which had "the best weather in SF." John traveled out from Seattle about a month ago to take advantage of having relatives who lived in Nairobi and had spacious accommodations to put folks up.

"So, do you have any hiking or trekking experience? How high have you gone?"

"I'm a hiker but only in the Cascades in the state of Washington." He wanted to know all about Everest and whether it was hard to get to Base Camp. So, I regaled him about my little team of two that had three Sherpas to hump our belongings to Mt. Everest. And yes, it was a bitch. But it was fun! Although this was the rainy season, we hoped that we might escape any showers on the upward climb. If lucky, we might get through the climb without any rain! But because we couldn't depend on it, we had rented a two-man tent just in case. Besides, it dropped very cold at night and a little extra protection was always welcome.

We checked in at the Naro Moru Gate road-head, at the start of the climb and we met our guides/porters. We had two porters. They were of the Kikuyu tribe from the surrounding area and their fathers and grandfathers had portered for the British. They said they would come by later to look at our provisions and would pack up the supplies. Because we were only doing three days, it was nothing like the supplies I had for my Everest climb. So, by 12 pm, we started at Naro Moru (7,874 ft) with our guides/porters heading to Met Station (10,000 ft). The first night, one sleeps in some comfort at one of the Met Stations log cabins. *Thank you, Kathy, for reserving our stay because you can't just expect that you can start climbing and find lodging.* Of course, this was the rainy season and in principle, there should be fewer people who want to climb outside the dry season. We got into Met Station around 4 pm. And our guides started cooking dinner. We could relax in the cabin and the fireplace had a roaring fire. This was very different from my Everest trek!

On Day Two, we asked for an early breakfast and to get started for a brisk walk from Met Station to Mackinder's Camp, which is at 14,000 ft. It took us five hours. We were prepared for the bog and to get mired down in the mud. But once you got to Teleki Valley, you had a spectacular view of the mountains. Tonight, we were roughing it in our pup tent. Even though 8 months previously I had trekked to the base camp Everest, this climb wasn't a walk in the park! I admit that I was tired, especially from the bog! I had prepared for Everest and read up on signs and symptoms of high-altitude sickness. Mt Kenya trekking was betting on a quick ascent and not allowing a lot of time to even develop altitude sickness. Fourteen thousand feet isn't that high and I remembered that it wasn't until 15,000 ft. in Nepal that I could feel the weight of lack of oxygen. We were turning in early around 5 pm. Tomorrow was the push.

The idea is that you want to get an early start. By early I mean they wake you up at 2 am to attempt to reach Point Lenana summit (16,400 ft) before the clouds obscure your view of the actual Mt Kenya. The standard trek for the inexperienced hiker is that you start in the darkness. I mean, it is pitch black. And by the time of the first light, your guide is cutting steps into the glacier for your ascent to Point Lenana. John and I were just climbing to the highest elevation where there was a lookout point to the higher peaks. Yes, we got there in time to see the sunrise in all its glory. I was ecstatic that we had gotten here without any symptoms. We only stayed about 40 minutes because the wind picked up and the clouds started forming. It was cold! Besides, we didn't want to push our luck. We made it; let's start down.

Going down was such a treat. We could practically fly. In 1 hour, we were at our camp at Mackinder's and one of the porters had a hot breakfast waiting for us. We did it! The rest of the day was just falling down the mountain. We wanted to get back to Nairobi before nightfall. It's surprising how fast you can descend when you want to. When we got down to the roadbed, we thanked our porters for the safe trip and paid them. My legs were feeling wobbly but with some stretching, they came back to life. We threw our equipment into the back of the Landcruiser and I started up the engine. Thank God it started right up. I noted that it had rained overnight at the lower elevation. I hoped the road was still navigable. We decided to forego lunch at Naro Moru and to keep on going until we could find a roadside place and grab something hot to eat. However, the road was treacherous. I hadn't noticed the incline on the ascent but with the wet and muddy road, the Landcruiser was slip-sliding around the steep curves even though I was already in the lowest gear. We rounded a curve and some people jumped out at us. I about had a heart attack. We finally came to a stop after sliding some ways. They were some ex-pats and they pointed to where their station wagon hadn't made the turn and was hanging by a thread with the back wheels hanging over the cliff and the front wheels just barely on the road.

"Shit, Marie," I said to no one.

"Can you pull us out?" they cried. I got a bad feeling in my stomach. We couldn't leave them in a lurch, but I heard Kathy's words in my head. *"Don't touch the winch!"* I didn't even know how to operate the fucking winch.

John looked at me and said, "Kathy won't get mad if you try to help them. It's an emergency."

"Fine, brother, but you're not the one she'll blame"! Fortunately, another SUV came down the mountain and one of their guides knew how to operate a winch. We manually pulled the cable and hook to the car and anchored the hook onto some bar underneath. I then got back in the jeep and turned on the engine. I got out the jeep book in the glove box and read the instructions.

Well, here goes nothing, I said to myself. And the winch started to slowly pull up the car. I was initially afraid that the car might cause us to be pulled down the cliff. But we had anchored the Landcruiser behind a big tree and if there were any sliding, the tree would prevent us from going over the side! Soon, we had a collection of six vehicles gathered around looking at us pulling the car up. I breathed a sigh of relief when it was on the road. Wild applause erupted. I wanted to cry. They offered to pay for this assistance. I just thanked the Lord and was happy to "pay it forward." You never know when you may need assistance!

Of course, John just couldn't wait to tell his sister about our adventure! Because the jeep wasn't totaled, we could have a great celebration. They would be off in two days for Home Leave. Kathy and Bob felt more at ease leaving me alone (with their staff) in their house. They were envious that I was planning a trip to Lake Turkana which was considered high adventure. They didn't feel bad about leaving me alone, since I seemed to be able to find solutions to any problems. I was going to miss my friends. They had shown me a whirlwind of a trip. I took the famous train from Nairobi to Mombasa to stay in a cabin on the beach for two weeks. We camped at Samburu while I learned to brave crossing streams in a Landcruiser. And John and I had a successful ascent to Mt. Kenya without any high-altitude sickness. They were sure I would survive the Lake Turkana Bus! And they invited their neighbor across the street, whom I met the first day I arrived in Kenya when I thought everyone had left for the beach, to join us for a barbeque. *Life can be very strange. I would meet Dr. Croft some 25 years later when I was posted in Nairobi in the USAID Regional Program and I sought treatment for my daughter, who was sick with some febrile illness.*

Not One Sound, Not One Motion

AS WE DROVE along the flat straight road to Battambang from Phnom Penh, my mind wandered back some thirty-five years earlier (1979). What was for me, at this moment, a relaxing, air-conditioned SUV ride north, was much different from the harried, furtive exit of Cambodians fleeing the urban centers like Phnom Penh or Siem Reap heading north.

. It must have been difficult back then, to avoid the bands of Khmer Rouge soldiers and I doubt that those fleeing north could take the most direct route. There wasn't much time to determine what to bring with them. So, they left priceless mementos behind, a treasured photo of parents, a well-loved piece of jewelry given by one's spouse as a part of one's dowry, a favorite book, now an item that would condemn one to death.

By the time my malaria team got to the "Thai-Cambodian border," it wouldn't be "my border" that would lead to Sa-Kaeo Camp some forty kilometers northwest just inside of Thailand. What was I doing in Battambang, Cambodia this February 2015? Ostensively, I was a member of a team that was tasked with developing a new malaria project for the U.S. Agency for International Development/ Cambodia. My real reason to join this expedition was to find closure to an episode at a Cambodian Refugee Camp in Thailand that had commenced in September 1979. I was working at the time for the Centers for Disease Control /Atlanta, the premier national public health institution for the United States. I was selected for their elite medical epidemiology (detective) investigative service, the *Epidemic Intelligence Service (EIS)*, and I had been sent as a first-year EIS officer to control infectious diseases in Sa-Kaeo Cambodian Refugee camp. I had long submerged my memories of those tumultuous days in some deep recesses of my mind.

This was my first visit to Cambodia (2015). It was exceedingly hot and muggy, the kind of weather that I abhorred but somehow always found myself consigned to work in. The landscape was surreal. At one time, this area had forests, thick forests. They have all been cut down and now there were barren rice fields waiting for the rainy season to come. Some of the team consumed a little too much of our morning tea and coffee, so we needed to find some public toilets. But there were no toilets in the rural areas as we well knew. I said, "let's just pull over to the side of the road, and we can take our chances just squatting down by some scrub bushes." And then we turned a bend in the road and one meter ahead on the right were three soldiers, backs to each other, waving these 60-inch metal wands in front of them right next to the road! And they weren't wearing any bomb-defusing suits either. We collectively decided that maybe, we could wait a little bit longer to reach the health center. *There were literally millions of landmines in Cambodia, still making huge swaths of terrain unusable to this day.*

Besides having unwanted landmines, this area of the Thai-Cambodian border also developed a resistant malaria parasite to the common treatment modalities. And it was worrisome because this very area thirty years ago had developed resistance to the first good malaria drug, chloroquine. And that resistance had spread to most areas of the world, including Africa, setting into motion a continuous search for newer and more effective drugs. Only problem though, is that each new drug never lasted long (on average 5-10 years), precipitating country programs to continually change their treatment protocols. We were being taken to interview some Village Malaria Workers (VMW) to see if these grammar school graduates would be able to manage an eradication program. We needed translators because these VMWs were under thirty years old and didn't speak the old colonial language, French. As we sat under the roof of the traditional wooden house on stilts, shaded from the sun beating relentlessly down on us, my mind drifted back to another time, and another place in Sa-Kaeo camp. At that time, I was trying to determine if the people who sat motionless in front of me were ill or just mentally devastated.

*Kampuchea (Cambodia) was proclaimed independent in 1953 after nearly 100 years of French colonization. Some 10 years of peace under the rule of neutralist Prince Norodom Sihanouk followed, but the country gradually became increasingly involved in the war in Southeast Asia. By the early 1970s, Kampuchea was the scene of extensive military conflict involving both internal and external factions. By April 1975 the **Khmer Rouge** (i.e., the Red Khmer) captured Phnom Penh and subsequently ruled the country, then called Democratic Kampuchea, for almost 4 years. The Khmer Rouge became notorious due to their policy of forced evacuation of the urban populations, resulting in much brutality and loss of life.*

Nearly fifteen years of intermittent military activity and changing government in Kampuchea led to social and political disruption, inadequate harvests, broken communications, and thousands of homeless people wandering in mosquito-filled rain forests. A Vietnamese invasion of Kampuchea in December 1978 was followed by the flight of the Khmer Rouge government from the capital toward western Kampuchea. By the spring of 1979, Khmer refugees of various political stripes began arriving in small numbers at holding centers run by the Office of the U.N. High Commissioner for Refugees (UNHCR) in Thailand and in larger numbers at camps on or near the Thai-Cambodian border. As fighting inside Kampuchea intensified at the beginning of the dry season in late September 1979, approximately 28,000 refugees were transported by trucks from the border to a rice field about 60 kilometers inside Thailand. This became the UNHCR holding center at Sa-Kaeo.

The devastating picture of exhausted civilians, dying children, crying mothers, and wounded of all ages provided the impetus for spontaneous humanitarian action. Hundreds of doctors, nurses, nutritionists, administrators, engineers, and relief specialists from many countries assembled quickly to help a large displaced population. Despite the enormity of the task and the inherent difficulties involved in coordinating many relief agencies and personnel with different languages, perspectives, and experiences, the relief operation was hastily implemented.

At the request of the Royal Thai Government, the International Committee of the Red Cross (ICRC) took charge of health-care activities and construction in Sa-Kaeo. The League of Red Cross Societies, a Geneva-based Red Cross umbrella group, arranged for many national Red Cross teams from several countries (including Thailand) to work under the leadership of ICRC to provide aide. In addition, many health workers were provided by various NGOs (non-governmental organizations). Issues concerning food, water, and administration were handled by UNHCR.

Initially, Sa-Kaeo was no more than a fenced-off area of bushland with no housing facilities, no water, and no sewage system. Part of the area was designated for the camp hospital. When the first refugees arrived, there were three doctors and eight other health workers with limited resources. Nearly 2,000 severely ill or dying refugees quickly overran the hospital area in the first few days. *By the time I arrived in the last week in September 1979, it was, in essence, a prison camp of barb wired fence surrounding the whole area. This was what the November 12, 1979 issue of **Time Magazine** on their front cover called "**Deathwatch in Cambodia**"!*

The Khmer Rouge subjected Cambodia to a truly radical social reform process that was aimed at creating a purely agrarian-based Communist society. The Khmer Rouge coerced around two million people from the cities to the countryside to take up work in agriculture. They forced people to leave their homes and disregarded normal, basic, human freedoms; they controlled how Cambodians acted, what they wore, to whom they could talk, and many other aspects of their lives. During their years in power, the Khmer Rouge killed many intellectuals, city-dwellers, minority people, teachers, and many of their own party members and soldiers who were suspected of being traitors. They wanted to eliminate anyone suspected of involvement in any *"capitalistic activities."* The Khmer Rouge believed that parents were tainted with capitalism, so they separated children from their parents, indoctrinated them in communism, and taught them torture. Children were a *"dictatorial instrument of the party"* and were given leadership in torture and executions. Was there any wonder why people were fleeing across the border to Thailand in 1979?

I arrived in Sa-Kaeo around September 22. It was a miserable, forlorn place. The camp was mistakenly built hastily in some sunken rice fields and the rainy season was ending. It was a sea of mud and mosquitoes. As I stood in the middle of the camp, *there wasn't one sound, not one person talking, not one crying baby, not one bird singing.* And this was in the midst of some twenty-eight thousand estimated refugees. Some were sitting in the mud, motionless. Others had barely made it under plastic blue tents. I was trying to get my bearings and figure out what I was supposed to do in this camp. I knew I needed a translator because Khmer wasn't one of my languages. I was hoping someone would approach me and miraculously speak both English and Khmer. But no one was moving. They were sitting skeletons; human beings more malnourished than I've ever seen. Too weak to even collect food handouts, much less prepare and cook them. Too weak to crawl to the hastily erected hospital wards 300 meters away.

The more I saw, the more disheartened I became. *Christ, I thought, What could I do here besides count the dead?* And then I heard a weak voice behind me, "Can I help you?" I turned to see a slender, short man who came up to my chest in height. *Someone wanted to help me?* I broke out smiling. "You speak English," I said excitedly.

"Yes, I need help. I'm a doctor, and I need someone to help me in my work controlling disease here."

"My name is Prem," he said softly, bowing with folded hands in front of his face. *"I worked in the U.S. Embassy in Phnom Penh. I speak English and French; I can work for you."* And from then on, my job became instantly more manageable.

I rapidly fell into a routine at the camp. As the resident epidemiologist, I was in charge of hunting down disease before it could take over the camp. Where did the water supply come from and was it safe? (Initially it was brought in by water trucks because there was no source of water close by). Later, wells were dug. How was sanitation handled? There were some pit latrines at the boundaries of the camp. *Shelter was still haphazard.* Some refugees were in tents while others were given reed mats and poles to construct traditional shelters. And the rainy season had not completely ended yet. I was obliged to manage two daily assignments every afternoon: **count the dead** (number of adult males, females, and children lumped together, sex not determined), **and present the mortality report** in the daily meeting of Heads of Relief Agencies and hospital wards. I also quickly needed to get consensus from the steering committee on how causes of death would be recorded. *Nothing too complicated*, so that we could eventually estimate a camp mortality rate. We agreed on eight or so categories with fever/malaria leading the bunch. The hospital's wards initially were just tents. Patients sprawled on the bare earth. There were no mats or beds. There was no paper to make patient charts and write mediations down. The camp had clearly opened hastily and was overwhelmed by the sheer numbers of severely ill patients.

During my second month at Sa-Kaeo in early November, the Camp Coordinator sent for me and handed me a message from the U.S. Embassy in Bangkok. Surprise! I was going to have a visitor. Her name was Rosalynn Carter! And I was to be her tour guide to show her the camp and what was being done for the plight of the refugees. Since I was the only person from a U.S. government organization, the Centers for Disease Control, I naturally came to mind to be her handler, facilitator, and translator.

Now I had many thoughts swirling through my mind at this unforeseen bit of drama. *Are they kidding?* The camp was a mess and not a place for show and tell. I had better things to do than escort the First Lady around. I went to the Thai Post Office and booked a midnight call to Atlanta. This was before cell phones and laptop computers! I returned to the Post Office at midnight.

"So, you got the news, Connie?" asked one smart ass. It appeared that the U.S. government wanted to show its concern for the plight of the Cambodians. Since I was the only government official there, I was nominated for the task, clear and simple. She was arriving in four days. *Great!* Then I will show her my Sa-Kaeo camp, with all the dirty laundry hanging out to see. *I will show her the real thing, no whitewashing.*

The camp was struggling to get an infrastructure in place and a system of triage to place critically ill patients into hospital wards. Besides malaria, most patients were severely anemic. An appeal went out to all health staff. *Could we donate a pint of blood?* I went into the makeshift lab and explained to the lab tech that normally my blood was never accepted in the United States because I had worked in malarious countries for the past ten years. Well, that wasn't a contraindication here! Did I have a hemoglobin of 14? They wanted my blood.

The important day arrived when the First Lady descended with a huge entourage of Embassy officials and journalists. My worst fears had materialized. This was going to be a circus unless I could circumvent this show somehow. I quickly introduced myself to Mrs. Carter, who seemed open but a little anxious about the whole experience. She was wearing a suit and inappropriate shoes to go walking in the perimeter mud with me. I explained that I could show her the camp and give an overview, but I didn't want hordes of journalists following us and taking pictures. I could take her on a walkabout and then deposit her back at the hospital and then the agency heads could explain the patients on their wards. So, while journalists and officials were settling down to get an overview from the camp coordinator, Hans Nordruft, I took Mrs. Carter for a short perimeter walk around the camp. One could get a good glimpse of what life was like for the so-called "healthy" refugees. Currently, there were about fifteen international and Thai health organizations that were providing health care in the camp.

Sa-Kaeo had a high proportion of Khmer Rouge fighters (you could easily spot the *checkered red and black krama (scarfs)* and the "tire sandals" sported by the Khmer soldiers. The civilian population was ostensibly under the soldiers' command. *Everyone still had that dazed "deer in the headlights look" and were listlessly crouching in front of their tents.* I explained how part of my job was traversing the camp and doing *surveillance* and identifying people who looked sick and should be in the hospital wards. I also was on the lookout for any new infectious disease that was striking people down. Then I delivered Mrs. Carter back to the hospital wards for the photo frenzy that ensued.

I thought I could relax somewhat after Rosalynn Carter left. But right away, the doctors on the hospital wards started reporting some strange symptoms in people who had initially evaded the wards. Adults were coming in with decreased muscle function, particularly in the lower legs, tingling or loss of feeling in the feet and hands, pain, mental confusion, difficulty speaking, vomiting, involuntary eye movement, and paralysis. Someone suggested we think of nutritional deficiencies. Displaced populations such as war refugees are susceptible to micro-nutritional deficiencies, including beriberi. And then we looked more closely at the food rations being provided to the Cambodians. Beriberi was endemic in regions dependent on what is variously referred to as *polished, white, or dehusked rice.* This type of rice has its husk removed to extend its shelf life, but unfortunately, it also has the unintended side effect of removing the primary source of thiamine. *Great, they survive the virulent malaria of the forests, and sidestep the landlines on the paths to Thailand, only to have the UNHCR cause a nutritional deficiency?* Urgent requests went out to find unpolished rice and to expedite delivery here!

We had barely gotten over the food emergency when there were reports of meningococcal meningitis. The first few cases came from the camp cluster composed of Pol Pot army recruits. I went to the small lab and asked the technician to see the smears. And as I looked in the microscope, I saw the tell-tale gram-negative diplococcus-*Neisseria meningitidis*. I quickly asked Hans to call the heads of organizations to prepare them for the next onslaught and see what antibiotics were available in the camp. We also needed to discuss how to prevent the spread of meningitis in the close, crowded camp. We needed to identify the location where the patient(s) came from and then convince the immediate cluster of people who lived with the patient to take preventive meds. We could technically vaccinate but there was only one problem: we didn't know the strain of the meningococcus, and we didn't have the A/C meningococcal vaccine available! Ampicillin was in short supply and the only drug in large quantities at the camp was a sulfa drug used back in the dark ages before penicillin.

So, the plan was for me to make a hasty map of the camp, identify where the patients lived, form a team of nurses to go out to give preventive treatment, to somehow identify those who received preventive meds, so we could later ascertain whether there was secondary spread among the preventive cohort. We only had gentian violet to use as a marker. There were all sorts of ill-advised suggestions like pinning paper badges on patients who got preventive treatment, which I shot down right away. So, we had them stick their right index finger in the gentian bottle after they swallowed the meds. We eventually had twelve cases of meningitis that were identified in four different locations around the camp. But because we quickly gave preventive meds to the family members and immediate neighbors, we stopped secondary spread!

Before I left Atlanta for Sa-Kaeo Camp, an old hand in humanitarian crises called me into his office. Wolf Bulle asked me if I had ever worked in a refugee disaster. I shook my head "no." He told me I would go through some definite mental health dilemmas and I needed to be prepared. I would be under high stress and initially, I would respond well to the emergency, working long hours, with little sleep and basically existing on the adrenaline of the moment. But after a week, I would become anxious and have insomnia and be unable to get the deaths out of my mind. Then because we were all so exhausted at the end of the day, we would have little time or energy to vent and support each other. We would sink into a depression. Colleagues would be hesitant to admit to this. *I needed to look for these phases, and to identify health workers who needed to take a "break."* I needed to give them "permission" to stay behind in their lodgings and to rest. *I needed to be alert to this condition in myself.* I began to note certain symptoms of anxiety and stress in staff by the second week. I would talk to the concerned person and just say I had been warned about these phases. Just talking would bring out a whole range of feelings from being overwhelmed, crying, a feeling of helplessness. I ordered them to take a break. They were to stay back at their lodging, walk to the market, go look for the beauty in nature. And then they could return to work, refreshed. And then I started to note these symptoms in myself.

For starters, I had the onerous task of counting the dead every day. The daily counts were high (250+ deaths daily) in the first two weeks with no signs of abating. I never had seen this many deaths in all my pediatric residency years! *It felt like we weren't making a difference.* Then, besides the high malnutrition rates, we were inundated with just a continuing series of outbreaks. First, we had the *cerebral malaria fiasco* that practically none of the hospital wards was initially treating successfully. I booked an urgent call at the Post Office again to CDC/Atlanta. Old hands at CDC said to fall back on *IV quinine* despite the dangers of administration, and provide plenty of hydration. I reported this treatment at the daily rounds of Heads of organizations and we finally started to see success on the wards. Then we had the beriberi epidemic and now we had the meningitis outbreak. People looked to the epidemiologist (me) to provide all the answers. I found I couldn't get to sleep at night, or if I did, I woke up with a start at 2 am wondering if the treatment was working. I was starting to get depressed.

So, I told my housemates that I was feeling under the weather and I would stay home that day. I walked into town and checked out the sights and tried to remove any thoughts about the refugee camp. I found a family run restaurant that had a live fish tank, and I picked out my lunch. *It was heavenly with the Thai spices.* I walked back home to my lodgings and pulled out my airplane book, which I hadn't touched since arrival. By the time my roommates arrived in the evening, I was feeling much better! I convinced them that we needed to go find that restaurant for some great Thai meals and a cold beer!

In the first two weeks I was at the camp, I was envious of the various Red Cross teams and the Israeli disaster team because they had a built-in support group. I was sent out solo. I knew how difficult it was to put in IVs in dehydrated patients, much less dehydrated pediatric patients. My residency training had been in pediatrics. So, I walked into the Israeli ward and offered my services to help start pediatric IV drips. Dr. Daniel W. on the Israeli team took me up on the offer, especially in those early weeks when patients lined the mats stretched so closely on the floor, and one could hardly navigate between them. After struggling on the ground inserting the IV needles and the saline drips, Danny would be sure to get me laughing about something before I left to visit the other wards. I would check into the triage tent to determine if any new disease was popping up. Each ward and their team operated independently, and there was no time for interaction with another ward when you had 120 patients to look after. So, if I found a team had instituted some innovation, I would note it, and mention it at the daily evening session with the steering committee.

A few weeks later, the situation had changed considerably. Water, initially brought into the camp by truck, was now provided by two deep wells that supplied a network of pipes throughout the camp. Trench latrines had been installed around the periphery of the camp, and refugees were taught to use them properly. General sanitation was improved by spraying insecticides, clearing rubbish, and draining stagnant pools of water. A 1,200-bed hospital, initially set up in large tents, was moved some weeks later into more permanent looking, solid, bamboo-thatch construction with gravel floors and septic tank-type toilets. Separate wards were designated for triage, pediatrics, obstetrics, intensive feeding, contagious diseases, and surgery.

The initial location of Sa-Kaeo in a swampy former rice field never improved, and the camp administration was forced to search for a better site. UNHCR chose six community leaders in the camp to show them the location of the new camp so they could squash any rumors about the move circulating to their groups. The leaders were at first reluctant to get in the vehicles to head to the site. They asked *if the lady epidemiologist was also going to the site*! So, Hans sent for me and asked me to join them. They were initially not comfortable going into the unknown, but if I were coming along, then it couldn't be that bad!

In late November, the camp was told they would be relocating. The steering committee decided to take advantage of the move and to take a census of the group to finally determine how many people were actually in the camp now. It also was an opportune time to vaccinate the children. We set up six stations of teams of nurses and doctors to provide immunizations, especially as we heard that Khoa I Dang, another larger camp on the border, had an outbreak of measles. The healthy refugees had to walk to the new location. When the refugees arrived at the new camp site, a new hospital had been constructed of bamboo with flooring and beds. Families had been asked to group themselves together in community groups, and they built their traditional bamboo structures. The camp took on the structure of a small village.

The medical steering committee grew more cohesive as the various health teams worked to provide a coherent health strategy. Sa-Kaeo had initial high mortality from fever/malaria. We found out more about this population; they had come from a central valley that had a hypo-endemic (low) exposure to malaria. As they traversed through the western mountains, they came into contact with a hyper-endemic (high) area of malaria and were exposed to resistant malaria in traversing the jungle. It took time to find out this information. I worked in Sa-Kaeo for ninety days, the allotted time that an EIS officer could work overseas on an outbreak. By the end of my stay, it was hard to even remember what the old camp was like. Life was transformed in the new Sa-Kaeo II camp. I learned so much from my international medical colleagues and from the Cambodians. They had gone through so much in Cambodia and their future was uncertain. Would they be returned to Cambodia or would some go on to a third country asylum?

As I walked through the camp on my last day, saying goodbye to the staff and to my faithful translator Prem, who had lost all his immediate family during the Khmer Rouge years, I wished I had heard something back from my mother. During my second month working in the camp, I wrote home to see if Mom could ask our Catholic parish if they would be willing to support a Cambodian refugee. I told Mom how helpful Prem had been to me. Without him in the camp, I wouldn't have been able to communicate with the people and to find out their concerns. Even though Prem was Buddhist, the parish could help him find a job and teach him how to maneuver through the reams of bureaucracy to find lodging. He even knew English! But letters take time to get to the states. And Mom had to present the idea to the parish council.

Now, I never told Prem that I had done this. I didn't want to get his hopes up. *And I hadn't received any mail back from my mother.* Actually, my mail was usually going in only one direction. I sent weekly letters, so my family could know I was safe and well. I started this practice from my Florence days in Europe. Since I hadn't gotten any mail before my departure, I felt I couldn't say anything to Prem. I paid Prem his last "salary" that came from my per diem money that supported me in Thailand. "I will miss you Prem. You were a vital part of my team. Without you, I would have been next to useless." And we bowed one last time with folded hands in the traditional Cambodian way. He taught me patience, acceptance, and compassion. I often wonder where he finally ended up. *Did he return to Cambodia or was he able to apply for asylum in the states? That is a question I have never been able to resolve to this date.*

Nowhere in Somalia

I WAS BACK in Atlanta in Viral Diseases Division following up on domestic outbreaks of diarrheal disease caused by the Norwalk virus. The phone rang and I was asked to go down to the Field Epidemiology Unit. *Now what?* I thought. The Chief of the unit indicated I should sit down.

"Connie, CDC has been requested to conduct a nutritional survey in Somalia," he said. "We want you to lead the team!"

"I'm interested, but I don't know anything about conducting nutritional surveys!"

"Don't worry, you can start training tomorrow."

But first I needed to find out more about the situation in the Horn of Africa. The University of Michigan was having a conference about the conflicts in the Horn of Africa, so our proposed team was sent to the conference to get up to speed.

Since the beginning of the 20th century, the concept of *Greater Somalia* started to develop with the birth of the nation of Somalia, as a united country inhabited by all the Somali clans in their "Horn of Africa" areas. Pan-Somalism refers to the vision of reunifying these areas to form a single Somali nation. *The pursuit of this goal has led to conflict*. If you remember only one thing, it is this! Somalia engaged in a war after World War II. *The Ogaden War* with Ethiopia was fought over *Ethiopia's* Somali Region and supported Somali insurgents against Kenya. In 1946, the Somali Youth League selected Harar as the future capital of Greater Somalia and subsequently sent delegates to the United Nations office in Mogadishu to reveal this proposal.

British Somaliland became independent on 26 June 1960 as the State of Somaliland, and the Trust Territory of Somalia (the former Italian Somaliland) followed suit five days later. On July 1, 1960, the two territories united to form the Somali Republic. On 15 October 1969, while paying a visit to the northern town of Las Anod, Somalia's then President Shermarke was shot dead by one of his bodyguards. His assassination was quickly followed by a military coup d'état on 21 October 1969 (one day after his funeral), in which the Somali Army seized power without encountering armed opposition—essentially a bloodless takeover. The coup was spearheaded by Major General Mohamed Siad Barre, who, at the time, commanded the army.

In Ethiopia, a predominantly rural society, the life of peasants was deeply rooted in the land, from which they eked out a meager existence. It has been this way through countless centuries. They have faced frequent natural disasters, armed conflict, and political repression, and, in the process, they have suffered hunger, community disruption, and death.

Periodic crop failures and losses of livestock often occur when the seasonal rains fail or when unusually heavy storms cause widespread flooding. It's a curious paradox! It's a given that pastoral nomads have to move seasonally in search of water and grazing, and they are often trapped when drought inhibits rejuvenation of the denuded grasslands, due to their overgrazing habits. During such times, a family's emergency food supply diminished rapidly, and hunger and starvation become commonplace until weather conditions improve and livestock herds are subsequently rejuvenated. For centuries, this has been the customary pattern of life for most Ethiopian peasants. Insurgent movements in Eritrea, Tigray, and the Ogaden have only served to exacerbate the effects of these natural calamities.

The Ogaden War was a Somali military offensive between July 1977 and March 1978 over the disputed Ethiopian region of the

Ogaden, and it began with the Somali invasion of Ethiopia. The Soviet Union disapproved of the invasion. When the USSR, found itself supplying both sides of this war, they attempted to mediate a ceasefire. When their efforts failed, the Soviets abandoned Somalia. All aid to Siad Barre's regime was halted, while arms shipments to Ethiopia were increased.

For the Barre regime, the invasion was perhaps the greatest strategic blunder since independence, and it weakened the military. Almost one-third of the regular Somali soldiers, three-eighths of the armored units, and half of the Somali Air Force (SAF) were lost. The weakness of the Barre administration led it to effectively abandon the dream of a unified Greater Somalia. The failure of the war aggravated fierce discontent within the Barre regime! The first organized opposition group, the Somali Salvation Democratic Front (SSDF), was formed by army officers in 1979. Now did we really need the two poorest countries in the Horn of Africa to be fighting? But since the Soviets decided to meddle in the Ogaden War, and throw their support to the Ethiopian regime, Ethiopia cut ties with the United States. *That led, of course, to the United States adopting Somalia as a Cold War ally from the late 1970s to 1988 in exchange for use of Somali bases, and as a way to exert influence upon the region.*

By mid-1980 most observers considered the refugee crisis in the Horn of Africa to be the world's worst. During the 1980s, the crisis intensified, as 2.5 million people in the region abandoned their homes and sought asylum in neighboring countries. Drought, famine, government repression, and conflict with insurgents were the principal causes of large-scale refugee migrations. But there were other factors: such as resettlement and the ill-thought-out *"villagization program"* in Ethiopia, conflicts in southern Sudan, and hostilities in northern Somalia, which also generated refugees. Sudan's war against the Sudanese People's Liberation Army (SPLA) forced many Sudanese into Ethiopia. In northern Somalia, the Somali National Movement (SNM) had been fighting Somali government forces, and in the process, hundreds of thousands of Somalis fled into Ethiopia.

So, this was the complex humanitarian situation facing my team heading into Somalia. Siad Barre made himself head of a Supreme Revolutionary Council and imposed autocratic rule through a personality cult and the harsh enforcement of an official ideology called "Scientific Socialism." He initially *officially outlawed clan loyalties* (while simultaneously using clan elders to establish order in rural areas) and promoted literacy with a newly introduced Roman alphabet. He later renounced his ties with the Soviets and sought U.S. aid, but allegations of human rights abuses hurt his international standing.

Sometime in mid-1980, journalist reports about the starvation of Ethiopian refugees in Somalia, led to pressure on the U.S. Congress to provide food aid to the refugees. Leaders in Congress pushed back that there was no starvation. However, the photos and journalist stories of the refugees created such a stink that Congress passed the buck and called on the CDC/Atlanta to send a team to do a nutritional survey and to uncover the true situation. So, our team of three headed off to Mogadishu. We were being seconded to the World Health Organization (WHO) to work under the Somali Ministry of Health. WHO would provide us vehicles, a driver, and a nurse/translator. We would be in the capital for a week, consulting with other UN organizations and NGOs. Then the team would touch base with the U.S. Embassy and let them know our plans.

I was the only person on the team currently based in Atlanta, so I met with the nutrition division to discuss the basic methodology. I would be packing three wooden measuring boards for measuring children under five mostly lying down. I would also have special weighing seats to hang children under three years old to get an accurate weight. Dr. Ron W. was the EIS officer in Michigan and he would make his way to Mogadishu separately. The third team member, Mr. Carl H. was a public health officer at CDC and had worked in several big disasters. The initial plan envisioned splitting up the team, with each person evaluating a different region and going into the field for a month. Then we would return to the capital, put all our data together, and analyze it. We would call in the results and get feedback on the basic data before presenting it to the MOH and WHO.

I would be carrying the important equipment and would transit Cairo on my way to Mogadishu. I think I had a 12-hr. layover in Cairo. And WHO was arranging a hotel in Mogadishu and would pick us up at the airport. Once again, I was heading for a hot, desert area, and the culture was fundamental Islamic, Sunni branch. There were four major clans in Somalia (Darod, Hawiye, Dir, and Rahaweyn) and many medium-to-small groups. Each clan could be further divided into innumerable subclans that consisted of tens of thousands of people alone. Within these subclans, there were even more group divisions based on kinship alliances of smaller extended families. Because of continuous past clan fighting, *President Siad Barre had forbidden everyone to ask or to talk about their clan under pain of punishment.*

My first impression of Mogadishu was of a sleepy Indian Ocean capital that operated on a slow time clock. The day I arrived, I finally met the rest of my team and we had a chance to talk and discuss our proposed itinerary. Our first week would be making the rounds of the UN agencies and gathering as much data as possible. We also went over team logistics. We needed to be clear on the methodology for conducting the survey and to decide which regions we would choose to get an idea of the magnitude of the problem. After discussions with the various UN agencies and key nongovernmental organizations (NGOs), our team selected the regions of Hiran (central), Hargesia (northwest, in former British Somaliland), and Gedo (south) in which to conduct the nutritional surveys.

We met our three national teams, each consisting of a driver and a nurse/translator, and we started to make lists of what we needed to take with us. If there were a famine, there wouldn't be a lot of food in the interior. We decided to buy pasta (spaghetti) and tomato sauce, long a staple in the region as Somalia was a colony in Italian East Africa. We tossed in a basket filled with grapefruits which could survive the harsh climate for weeks and provide some vitamin C. We needed to take sufficient jerry cans of petrol, not knowing the situation in the interior. And don't forget sufficient water rations; a lesson learned the hard way when I ran out of water in the Thar Desert of Rajasthan during smallpox eradication days! (1975).

We worked with the UN to make rough maps of where to find displaced persons and refugees, and the UN supplied the locations of NGOs providing humanitarian assistance. The team agreed to rendezvous in the capital after 25 days. We would then analyze the results. Before leaving, we thought it best to move to a more economical Somali hotel with a good reputation that could keep our supplies. We found one near to the ocean, and its owner, Amina, was known for making the best Somali tea!

Every evening while we were in the capital, we would hit up a different restaurant along what was called the Lido Beach and order lobster or another shellfish. There was a small Somali fishing community, but the Somalis didn't actually eat the fish. They were a goat and camel eating community, so the price for lobster was really cheap. At that time in October 1980, there was a heavy UN and NGO presence in Mogadishu, so despite Somalia being a Muslim country, there was a sprinkling of nightclubs in a certain quarter of the city. We thought to go and listen to some music and eat a good meal before leaving for the interior.

Early on when I arrived, I admired the Somali women's national dress. At that time in the capital, they didn't wear the full body covering of the burka. When I traveled to a new post, I always liked to get the national dress to blend in with the people. So, early in our stay I ordered a Somali dress from one of the many tailors in the market. For our last night together before taking off, the team wanted to enjoy ourselves. We would be leaving right after breakfast. I talked again with Amina about us keeping our rooms and that I was concerned that none of the rooms had keys to lock them. She assured me that wouldn't be a problem.

The notion of honor (*sharaf*) is central to Somali culture. Personal honor is deeply intertwined with family reputation in Somalia, regardless of wealth or power. Traditionally, one's behavior would affect the honor or reputation of the entire clan or community. There was a very strong community focus embedded in Somali culture. People are mutually reliant on their family and community for support to meet essential needs. Dependence upon kin had become particularly crucial to survival since the civil war. The government's capacity to provide basic services or respond to humanitarian or conflict-related disasters was low. Therefore, Somalis relied on their kin to provide food, protection, and conflict resolution. Everything was always redistributed and shared among the community, from engagement money to compensation money. One's community also took responsibility for an individual's actions. For example, if a person commits an offense, traditionally, their kin group is held responsible and must pay compensation. *So, I wasn't worried. Our things would be where we left them.*

We had been given the name of a nightclub that had a great reputation of having good food and great music. The place was primarily frequented by UN expats and it was packed. We had a relaxing evening, and I got several compliments on my Somali dress. It was almost 11 pm and time to walk back to our hotel. We had a long day tomorrow. Having a Somali hotel in the central district was convenient and everything was close. You didn't need a car to get around.

We were leisurely strolling down the street, which was literally deserted. We stopped in front of the Russian Embassy, looking at some photos and laughing about something. In the distance, I heard and felt the rumble of a huge military truck coming down the street. We looked up and wondered what it was doing slowly creeping down the street. I suddenly got a terrible feeling in my stomach.

The truck screeched to a halt, and two soldiers jumped down with drawn assault rifles.

I stepped forward and shouted, *"You're making a big fucking mistake!* I'm not Somali! So, get right back on that truck and keep on going!"

My male companions stared at me, speechless!

"Sorry, sorry," said one of the soldiers and motioned to the other one to back up. They jumped into the cab of the military truck and they sped off down the street.

"What the hell was that?" yelled Ron.

"You're not going to believe this!" I told them about this private briefing I had right before leaving for Somalia with Dr. Wolfe Bulle, a well-known humanitarian who worked for thirty years with various NGOs. He was putting together briefing packets for CDC/Atlanta for different Asian and African countries, as to the cultural and religious sensitivities one needed to work in other cultures. The Centers for Disease Control and Prevention sent numerous epidemiologists out to work on disease outbreaks, and the briefing documents were to help orient people "new" to disaster situations and be prepared to cope with the inevitable culture clash.

Lab and infectious disease specialists had briefed us as to the diseases we would encounter. We also discussed at length how we would conduct the nutritional survey and the methodology. So, I had no clue as to why Wolfe wanted to see me.

"Connie, I know you have the briefing packet on Somalia, so you can read up on particular customs at your leisure. I just wanted to alert you to something fairly new that won't be in the briefing material," Dr. Bulle said. "I recently heard something from a friend who just got back from a UN assignment in Somalia."

And then he proceeded to tell me some worrisome information.

"What I'm going to say wouldn't pertain to a white woman epidemiologist going over there, but you know you look like a Somali woman."

He continued to tell me that the UN and various Western NGOs have been in Somalia addressing the humanitarian situation. Western men have appreciated the beauty of the Somali women and have been going out with them. Apparently, the Somali government—which was conservative and Muslim—wasn't happy "their" women were seeing foreign men. They couldn't exactly kick out Western aid, because they did need it. They couldn't exactly beat up the men, which might cause an international scene. But they could put pressure on their women. The military was going around late at night, and if they saw a Somali woman out with a Westerner, they picked her up, tossed her into a truck, and took her to jail. After a five-day stay in jail, harassment, and a little beating, the women were warned not to continue to go out with foreigners, or else . . .

"Just be careful. Stay alert."

I thanked Bulle for the heads up.

"So, when that military truck started down the street," I told my companions, "I knew there would be a confrontation. I had five seconds to make them believe I was American and back off! Fortunately, they did!" We walked a little quicker to the Somali hotel. That night, as I was drifting off to sleep, I reflected that maybe I should reevaluate my penchant to "blend in" with the culture.

So, my team was to go to Hiran Region to a town called Beledweyne. Ronnie, was heading south to Gedo Region. And Carl was heading north to Hargeisa. Beledweyne is a city in central Somalia. Located in the Beledweyne District, it's the capital of Hiran province. The town is situated in the Shebelle Valley near the Ethiopia border, some 210 miles (345 km) north of Mogadishu. Beledweyne is divided by the Shebelle River into eastern and western sections. A Swedish team of ten people had established disaster relief operations in the area and established their camp. The UN contacted them by radio and explained my goal. They agreed to put me up in their camp! I was excited since that meant I would have some human contact. They could put me up but not my whole team. My national team could find lodgings in the District headquarters. I inquired how I was to find their camp and the UN said, "Go north out of the capital until the paved road peters out. Then turn north-west and look for the terrain to turn semi-arid with masses of acacia trees. If we crossed over into Ethiopia, we had gone too far. Soon we were just following a track.

It's a long, hot drive to Beledweyne and so we had ample time to exchange family histories. My team was interested in my family, so I aimed to please. Then I turned to them and asked, "So, what clan am I from?" And I winked in saying it. At first, there was a stunned silence, since I knew it was politically incorrect to discuss or ask anyone what their clan was. I don't know why I did that. I think I was trying to break down barriers, but we all know how things can go haywire when you tell jokes or try sarcasm in another language. *Most times, it doesn't work.* But my team looked at me, laughed, and said, "You're my clan!" and we moved on.

We got to Beledweyne some six hours later and asked in town where the Swedes were located. They had taken over a former landholder's enormous house that had a large salon, kitchen, and multiple large bedrooms that had a profusion of beds tucked in every nook and cranny. I introduced myself to the Director of the team who welcomed me into the fold. If I didn't mind helping to wash up the dishes or cooking, I was invited to share with them. The Swedish team had been in Hiran for about a month and there were around six refugee camps spaced out in the province. They could draw me a map. They had several doctors, nurses, a water and sanitation specialist, along with those doing supplemental feeding. They invited me to use their house as a base and go out to various refugee camps to do my nutritional surveys. They weren't the only team in the province. About a mile away was also a French humanitarian team. So, I picked their brains and started asking a million questions. My national team went off to search for lodgings in town.

After an orientation by the Swedish Director, I talked to my team about where we should start to conduct the study. We went by the District Health Office (DHO) to check in and to let them know we would be working in the camps. The DHO informed me to alert the camp administration before starting the nutritional survey. We were to find the camps by going west and turning at the first acacia tree. And off we went. We caused a mild sensation on arrival, since so few vehicles came out to this refugee camp composed of a ragtag collection of *arquls* (traditional huts) hastily thrown up. I needed "assistants" to help with the survey, so I selected four young men, eager to accompany us throughout the camp and help in weighing and measuring the children. Once a hut was selected by the agreed formal methodology laid down by CDC, I had to make sure that they showed us all their children under five. They tended to "hide" children who were disabled or very malnourished, since it was a sign that the community wasn't taking care of them well. Once the team understood the process, we started working fast and well. But I could see that it would take several days to complete the survey in the camp.

My team of young men—I guessed they were in their late 30s—were curious and eager to learn everything about this foreign lady. Surprisingly for me, the Somalis were very friendly. Rather than having "acquaintances," Somalis generally see everyone as their friends. Once a Somali has met somebody, they are usually prepared to open their homes and lives to that person and help them in times of need. It is similarly expected that the new person would be willing to do so in return. This quick development of personal relationships can be very different from Western notions of privacy. Sometimes, their openness to converse can come across as quite direct or bold to those from the English-speaking West. For example, it's normal for a Somali to directly approach a stranger for a chat. Many Somalis report that they miss this aspect of their culture while living overseas. *They often describe how strangers in Somalia are met with a very welcoming and open attitude that they do not necessarily experience in Western countries.*

Somalis tend not to think conservatively about the future, but rather give what they can to others now. Therefore, people can often rely on the hospitality of strangers. For instance, a person may be able to travel long distances across Somalia without comprehensive provisions as they will be taken care of by the strangers they come across on their journey. It made me think back to my smallpox days in India when a village killed their one and only chicken to feed my team. But the issue for me was that this village was poor as a church mouse and some of their children were bordering on the moderately malnourished. I felt that I was taking food from the mouths of their children. So, after this experience, I had my team tell villagers that I was allergic to eggs and chickens and not ever to offer them to me. Just one taste and I would have an anaphylactic shock and die!

One time my team left very early in the morning because we needed to find a different camp. We decided to stop at this village and get some breakfast. I was busy watching the guy prepare this liver concoction (okay, I'm not usually a fan of liver!) and I noticed an exchange of heavy bargaining or so I thought between my driver and someone in the village. My driver had this great curved knife that had a wonderful scabbard. And I could see this other guy was really enthralled with it. And then after about a 10-minute discussion, my driver just gave the knife to this guy! I was astonished and afterward asked my driver, "Did you know this guy, or is he a long-lost relative because your knife is your prized possession?"

He said, "No, I just met him, but his clan is close to mine. He really admired my knife and I wanted him to have it. So, I offered it to him." In Somalia, people generally extend an offer multiple times. It's expected that you politely decline the gesture initially, before accepting on the third offer. This exchange is considered polite as the insistence to extend the invitation shows *hospitality* and the initial refusal to accept shows *humbleness*, and that one isn't greedy. Be sure to offer everything multiple times in return. If you only offer something once, a Somali may respond, "No, it's okay," out of modesty and politeness, even though they intend to accept on the third offer.

Westerners have to be very careful when you compliment an item in a Somali's house, as they may feel compelled to offer it to you as a gift. If they try to give it to you, insist that you appreciate their gesture but don't want to take it. A Somali is likely to offer the object out of politeness, and if you accept, they may end up giving you something they wished to keep.

Once, when my team was driving somewhere, I saw my nurse/translator admiring my sapphire ring from a distance. I said, "Now, here's the difference with American culture. I don't care how much you admire my ring, but I'm not going to give it to you!" And then we all broke out laughing.

So, we were finishing up the survey in our first camp in Hiran, and it was about 2 pm. A person ran up to one of my camp assistants and whispered something hurriedly in his ear. He dropped everything, came up to me, and said, "Dr. Davis, you have to leave now, right now! You are in danger!" I looked around and didn't see anything out of the ordinary, but I saw in the corner of my eye that my jeep was swiftly coming through the camp. My team quickly got all our equipment folded and thrown into the jeep and we said our goodbyes hurriedly. Then my driver took a wide turn around the camp and we left in an unusual direction. Then in the distant corner of the camp I could see there was some disturbance and a crowd of about 100 angry people appeared to be yelling and shaking their fists before the camp administration. I couldn't figure out what was going on. Neither could my team. We had been working each day in the camp with no problem. I told the driver to head back to the District Health Office because we needed to find out what was going on.

When we got back to the main road, we still had about an hour to get back to the district capital. Then we suddenly noticed on some cliffs to the right a mob of people who seemed to be angry. And then they started throwing these large boulders down on us! I mean very large stones were raining down that if they crashed into our vehicle, we could be goners. These villagers were lined up along the cliff for about a half of a kilometer. There was a lengthy trailer truck ahead of us that was weaving back and forth across the road to outwit the people throwing stones. Then my driver pulled out and went to the outside of the truck. He positioned our jeep to keep protected by the truck so the stones would first hit the truck and not us. As we finally got away from that section, we pulled ahead and sped off. I was very frightened and confused. "Head to the District Health Office, I said."

I jumped out of the jeep in front of the office and ran up the steps. I rushed into the DHO's office crying out "What's going on? There are mobs on the cliffs throwing boulders and, in the camp, we were warned to leave immediately!"

The DHO told me to sit down. "I'm glad you're not hurt!" And then he recounted that the camp refugees were upset about the food rations. A recent supply had brought in some flour that they all hated. This flour was a new shipment that arrived on some boat from Norway and was part of the Food and Agriculture Organization (FAO) food shipment. The people were complaining about the smell and the taste! They were refusing to touch it. The DHO had a sample and I said, "Give me some. I'll take it back to my house and prepare some biscuits with it." I wanted to understand what the problem was. When I finally got back to the Swedish house and looked at the flour, I could begin to understand.

> For starters, there was a faint odor, kind of a fishy smell. It wasn't pungent, but I could detect the slight odor of fish. I found some butter and powdered milk and made a small batch of biscuits. I tasted them. They were okay, certainly not Aunt Jemimah's biscuits but acceptable to me. Yes, there was a faint fishy taste, but you could barely detect it. Well, I guess this flour didn't make an acceptable "injera," a white leavened Ethiopian bread made from teff flour, similar to a crêpe. The refugee camp was having no part of it. Norway had made

this flour from dried fish. But Somalis, especially Somalis who lived primarily in the interior, had never tasted fish and didn't want to start now! The UN had to make frantic calls to Europe to try and expedite an emergency shipment of wheat flour from somewhere. The DHO told me to lie low for several days and not go out to any of the camps until this simmered down! Hey, I could do with several days of vacation, so no skin off my nose. The big festival of EID was coming up.

Africa is home to over 5 million people who follow the Islamic faith, with the Middle East and North Africa (MENA) region having the highest concentration of Muslims worldwide. The majority of the continent's Muslims live in North, West, and East Africa, with over 90% of the population in Algeria, Libya, Mauritania, Egypt, Djibouti, Gambia, Senegal, Morocco, Niger, Sudan, Somalia, and Tunisia following the Islamic faith.

Over 70% of the Nigerian population is Muslim, and in Ethiopia, Kenya, and South Africa, Muslims account for 50%, 33%, and 3% of the population, respectively. Eid al-Fitr is considered a reward for Muslims who have completed the fasting and spiritual growth period of Ramadan, which is one of the five pillars of Islam. During Ramadan, believers refrain from eating, drinking, and sexual relations from dawn to sunset, and perform additional prayers, especially at night to be conscious and grow closer to God, as well as foster feelings of empathy (for the poor who don't have food to eat) and goodwill.

Ramadan usually lasts for 29 or 30 days, and it ends with the recital of the Takbeer, which is a prayer of praise to God. After Ramadan, Eid al-Fitr celebrations usually commence with prayer at the mosque, followed by sharing meals and gifts with family, friends, and the community. In a nutshell, Eid is filled with lots of eating, visiting with loved ones, and celebrating the end of the fasting month of Ramadan. My team expressed the feeling that "happiness is felt because we'll see our families, eat well, and be merry."

Since Eid was coming up, I talked to my team and said, "We should buy a big sheep for our survey assistants in the camp. They had looked out for us and warned us to leave before things got out of control. I know they don't have money to get normal supplies, and they're not near a mosque. It's the least we can do." So, we headed out to look for an animal market. I relied on my team to pick the best sheep. It was huge, and it took three people to flip it on its back, tie up its hoofs, and throw it into the back of the jeep. They also got some spices and we headed to the camp. We arrived about 10 am and we caused such excitement. Man, that sheep must have known what was going to happen because he messed up the back of the jeep big time! It took my poor driver two hours of hard scrubbing to get the inside cleaned up. In the meantime, I was being offered tea and needed to accept hospitality in each of the huts of my Somali assistants.

I also saw the halal killing and then the skinning and the roasting of the sheep. It was going to take all day, so I just settled down in one of the huts, and got to partake in another aspect of life in a refugee camp. Oh, the aroma of the roasting sheep. Just seeing the joy on their faces was enough thanks. It must have been a long time since they had celebrated like this. The sheep's preparation was the best I had ever tasted. After we had eaten, I was drinking tea and telling my team, "It's getting late and we should leave before nightfall." Our host said, "Wait, wait," and took me outside. In the distance, I saw a herder boy leading a very pregnant camel our way. It took a few minutes for it to dawn on me that I would be getting a present. By now there was a sizable crowd outside the tent. When the camel arrived, our host handed me the bridle and said the clan wanted to honor me and show their appreciation. Three times, they pressed on me the gift of the camel. I was really getting nervous. First, although everyone knew I loved camels, what was I going to do with a camel in the states? Yet, I didn't want to offend.

This camel was beautiful. She was a light, caramel-colored female and while not knowing the exact gestational age, it looked to me that she was going to have her calf anytime soon. So, I stood up and bowed, accepted the gift, and said, "I want you all to know how much I appreciate my gift. But I'm in a quandary. Where I lived in the states right now, there is no nearby pasture. I wouldn't be able to sufficiently take care of this precious gift. I would like to ask a favor, could they take care of my camel? One day I would return to see the mother and her calf. But right now, I couldn't take care of them." So, they accepted to guard my camel until I returned. *Somewhere in Upper Shabelle, I have two camels that are waiting for my return. I must remember that!*

PSS: I rejoined my CDC teammates back in Mogadishu after being out in the field for a month. We got down to serious work of analyzing the data from the three regions and I went to book a call back to Atlanta to give them the results. I reported our findings of severe malnutrition (24-28%) with the highest numbers in Gedo region. Atlanta initially didn't believe the data because it was the highest ever reported in the literature at the time. I was told to go back to the team and to recalculate our findings! We did. The calculations didn't change. When we eventually got back to Atlanta, I was sent to Washington D.C. to report *in person* to the Senate committee. *The journalists' reports were correct; food aid was desperately needed for the country!*

SAVOR THE TIME ALONE, GAIN VALUABLE INSIGHTS

I think Americans, as a people, like being surrounded by friends all the time. They have this need to "be busy." Yet, at times, one needs to take advantage of the time alone to think, relax, and plan. Alone time increases empathy.

When you spend time with a certain circle of friends or coworkers, you can develop a "we vs. them" mentality. *Spending time alone to meditate or just to "chill" can help you develop more compassion for people who may not fit into your "inner circle."*

Solitude increases productivity.

Although so many work places started creating open floor plans so everyone could communicate more easily, studies have shown that being surrounded by people kills productivity. *Turns out people perform better when they have a little privacy.* Of course, you normally don't have a say in how your office structure is laid out. Currently, we're existing in "the time of COVID-19" and we either have a job that can be performed remotely and safely or we're unemployed. This is going on 9 months in self-isolation. I'm in a part of Mexico that has a large retirement community. When the coronavirus pandemic started, the Canadian snowbirds who normally stayed in Mexico for five months during the winter, and then return to Canada for the summer, were only given one week's warning by their embassy to return home swiftly or be blocked from returning for an unspecified time. Most of my Canadian friends packed up and sped home. And Canada certainly handled the pandemic much better than the pathetic response displayed by the U.S. Administration of the time.

Those Americans who stayed around Lake Chapala voluntarily went into self-isolation and had to put up with competing and contradictory announcements from the Mexican Federal and State authorities. Scientific guidelines were indicated but then neither government authority followed what they preached. Initially, the strict lockdown kept out COVID-19 cases. But then after five months, when cases were still escalating in Guadalajara, the government relaxed restrictions. Now, there are many cases in the towns on the northern shores of Lake Chapala. Mexico is a cash society, and without any government stimulus checks, the people have a stark choice: find work or starve. Not a great choice.

And for the retirees, we miss interaction with our friends and yearn for the pre-COVID-19 days. The first two months, I wallowed in self-pity but then, I finally realized that this time was a gift. I could write my next book! So, I got down to business.

Solitude sparks creativity.

There's a reason a lot of authors or artists dream about wanting to go to a cabin in the woods or a private studio to work. Being alone with your thoughts gives your brain a chance to wander, which can help you become more creative.

Being alone can help you build mental strength.

We're social creatures and we need to have strong connections with other people. But solitude may be just as important. Studies show the ability to tolerate alone time has been linked to increased happiness, better life satisfaction, and improved stress management. *People who enjoy alone time experience less depression.*

Being alone allows you to plan your life.

Most people spend a lot of time planning weddings and vacations but never plan how to get the most out of life. Spending time alone can give you a chance to ensure there's a purpose to all your hustling and bustling. Quiet space can provide an opportunity to think about your goals, your progress, and the changes you want to make in your life.

Solitude helps you know yourself.

Being alone helps you become more comfortable in your skin. When you're by yourself, you can make choices without outside influences. And that will help you develop more insight into who you are as a person.

You Need to Be Enterprising About Creating Time to Be Alone

If you find yourself daydreaming about being alone on a deserted island, I'm going to bet you aren't incorporating enough alone time into your life.

Set aside a few minutes each day to be alone with your thoughts; even just 10 minutes a day can help. Silence your electronics and allow your mind to wander.

If you aren't used to solitude, it can feel uncomfortable at first. But creating that quiet time for yourself could be key to becoming the best version of yourself. *And just maybe the best version of yourself is risking pushing yourself to dare to go outside your comfort zone. Dare to experience something you've never done before!*

Hitchhiking in Norway

❧

THE MAGICAL JUNIOR *Year Abroad* in Florence was ending. I experienced so much. It was hard to think that the year was rapidly ending, and I would be returning to the United States. I wondered if it would be a letdown for me. Europe was just so intoxicating, and I wanted it never to end. So, I begged my parents to let me prolong the year and to hitchhike through Scandinavia with two women from Gonzaga in Florence. I only needed five dollars a day I begged. Do you remember those days when you could travel through Europe on $5 a day? And they said yes! So, at the end of the closing tour of France and England for our student group, I was waiting for the ferry in Newcastle heading to Bergen, Norway. I was traveling with two Gonzaga in Florence buddies who studied with me. The plan was to hitchhike through the Scandinavian countries of Norway, Denmark, and end up in Sweden. And then fly from Sweden to London. We were taking a month for this and would be able to take a later crossing of the MS Aurelia, the Italian ship back to New York. We planned to stay in youth hostels, so this adventure would be economical.

The ferry docked on time in Bergen and we didn't waste any time in getting to the main highway. We were traveling with backpacks and had left our suitcases in London at the hotel to which we would return. We immediately got a lift from someone who was going about an hour down the road to some little village. I forget the town we were heading to but we planned to get in early around

4 pm because we still needed to get to the hostel. In those days (1965) most hostels weren't in the main towns but located at some distance from them in a rural area. Our last ride had dropped us on a crossroads that was just a short distance from the main town, but it was about five miles to get to the hostel. We had eaten a heavy lunch so weren't hungry just tired from getting up early to catch the ferry in Newcastle. The sun had started to go down somewhat earlier than expected.

It gets a little cool just standing in the shade. Surprisingly, no cars were passing on this road. Strange. I wondered why they place the hostels so far from the main town, but it probably has to do with getting a cheap property to rent. Julie said, "Maybe we need to start walking to the town. There hasn't been a car for one hour. If we start now, we can probably arrive in about another hour. We'll have to look for a place to stay and, according to our hostel book, we would need to get a hotel." This wasn't what we planned. Damn, this trip wasn't starting off right. But what to do? I had been dreaming of a warm lodging, so I was jerked back to the present. Just as we shouldered our packs a car approached. Crap, it was a police car. The sergeant saw us and pulled over. He guessed, correctly, that we spoke only English. "Hello," he said. What are you doing here?" We said, "We're trying to get to this hostel which is supposed to be up this road."

He shook his head and said, "Few cars take this road at night. You need to come to the main town because the hostel is still some distance." I spoke up, "But we planned on staying in hostels; we can't afford to stay at hotels. We're heading for Stockholm eventually. Are there any cheap hotels in town?" He looked at us and shook his head. "Best to put your packs in the trunk and get in the car." We obeyed silently.

Once in the police car, we talked among ourselves that we best readjust our thoughts about staying in hostels. We had to get to them by 3 pm, or we'd be over budget if we ended up staying in hotels. The police car pulled up to the police station. The officer turned to us and said, "You can stay in jail tonight. I only ask that you leave by 7 am." We walked into the jail. He unlocked the cells. We were free to use the showers, and I took the opportunity to also wash out my underwear. As I stood in the shower and let the hot water pour over me, I reflected on the situation. I had never actually been to a police station in the United States. Police were people to be avoided. He really didn't have to offer to take us into town. He certainly didn't have to offer to put us up. It was his demeanor and openness. He heard us discussing how we needed to change our approach and get into places early to be sure that we could get to hostels. We weren't treated like criminals. I thought about if we three hitched in the States, what would the response be, if any, to being stranded out on a lonely road. I wish now that I had asked him why he was helping us.

We crashed early. We were up by 6 am and packing up. We thanked the officer who saved us from shelling out money for an unplanned hotel. And we learned the hard way to always make it to the next hostel well in advance of nightfall. We walked to the end of the town to start hitchhiking. We got a lift immediately, but he was only going to the next town. For being a main road through the country, there still weren't a lot of cars. We had already passed my hitchhiking limit of "only waiting no more than ten minutes" time! A woman came out of the house and said, "come in and get a snack, it's a little chilly this morning." We thankfully accepted her kind offer. She made us some scrambled eggs and the coffee hit the spot. She indicated that traffic would pick up in the late morning but doubted if we would get a ride all the way to Sweden. It was a pleasant interlude and we thanked her and said we better get back out on the road.

Then several cars came down the road. Surely one will stop. And it did! It pulled over and a young guy in his early thirties got out. This was a new occurrence. Turns out that he was a reporter! He was interested in what three beautiful women were doing on the main road and where we were headed. We gave him a story, but I was disappointed that we weren't advancing toward Oslo.

He took our photo, and I didn't think much about it because a car came down the road and we had a direct ride all the way to Oslo! Nevertheless, you will be hard-pressed to believe this, but sometimes fact is stranger than fiction. When I returned to Gonzaga University for my junior year, I met a Norwegian student who was living in the foreign students' house on campus. He asked me out for coffee and said he had something interesting to show me. I was curious. Then he pulled out a folded newspaper clipping and there, on the front page of this Norwegian newspaper was a photo of the three of us women hitchhiking and the article in Norwegian. What was the likelihood that I would meet someone with that article? *Chance occurrence? Or just plain luck!*

On the Trail to Everest

✤

TREKKING TO THE base camp of Mt. Everest had been an elusive childhood dream during my Girl Scout years. I was a member of an outdoor troop in the San Francisco Bay Area. One of the mothers taught us to rock climb with ropes. Another mother was a ski fanatic and invited the troop to their cabin and taught those of us skiing basics before going up to the slopes. When I had the chance to work in the World Health Organization's smallpox eradication program in India, I jumped at the prospect. On the off chance that I might be able to get some time off and go to Nepal, I threw my hiking boots and several thick woolen socks in my duffel bag. India was hot and humid, and I bought most of my clothes for working in the field in India because they were lightweight cotton and conformed to the standards of modesty. I threw in my lightweight down jacket. It came in handy later in the Rajasthan Desert.

After working 18 months of twelve-hour days, hunting down smallpox cases, I asked for some vacation time. I put out the word to my smallpox brothers in India to see if anyone wanted to trek to Everest. Lots wanted to go, but just getting time off was a problem. In India, we were down to one-digit outbreaks in areas that two years before had thousands of cases. Dr. Paul Rotmil, a junior doctor from Sweden, heard of my request and wrote to me that he always wanted to do the trek. He even had a trekking guidebook and could take time off also! He knew someone in the Nepal program and offered to contact them to get assistance with flights going from Kathmandu to Lukla. The important thing was to set the dates. We would meet in Kathmandu and book in one of the many backpacker hotels.

We knew we could get food and tent supplies in Kathmandu. I was worried about whether we could rent parkas and wool pants for the ascent. When I left for my posting in India, climbing to the Base Camp of Mt. Everest seemed like a farfetched idea that I seriously didn't think it was possible. I worried most about proper outerwear. I only had the lightweight cotton clothes from India. But there were several rental outfitter stores and you could also rent a kerosene stove, gloves, and other supplies for high altitude. Once in Nepal, we chatted up hikers who had just descended from the trek and got some valuable tips on choosing porters and guides and how much they cost. I read a lot about altitude sickness before leaving the United States, but specific tips on how to avoid its effects were few and far between.

Weather is always a confounding variable, especially since trekking in Nepal in the high country is confined to two very specific timeframes within which it was most feasible to actually hike to Base Camp. Paul and I had concerns about flying to the take-off point in Lukla since the weather was cloudy and overcast for the two days before our booked flight. If we couldn't start the trek on time, we might have difficulty even keeping up with the itinerary and returning in the allotted time.

I was surprised at the quality of the sleeping bags and outerwear that you could rent. My parka for example *supposedly* belonged to the first woman to scale Mt. Everest. I can attest that her parka was toasty warm, and I regret returning the parka instead of buying it. I should have kept it because I never came across another one quite like it! I bought the wool pants outright, because I thought after wearing them for 3 weeks continuously, the rental place might refuse to take them back. Paul and I had numerous experiences to share about tracking down rumors of persons with smallpox. We were both fit. Smallpox work necessitated walking a lot while doing contact tracing work. Katcha (dirt, bad) roads might get you close to the identified village, but to actually access it, you needed to walk! Granted, in both West Bengal and Rajasthan the terrain was mostly at sea level. How would my body react to high altitude? Would I be able to reach Base Camp?

At Lukla, we quickly selected our guide Sonnan Temba, who had a good knowledge of English. He also told us he portered with the Japanese women's team that had the first woman to scale the mountain. I figured we would have good storytelling on the way up. With our team of three Sherpas (guide, and two heavy lifters) we started up the trail. During the first five days, we would stay overnight with the families of the Sherpas as we passed by their houses so they could gather their gear and food provisions. It was late October, so this would probably be their last trip on the mountain this year.

At the start of the journey, I didn't realize how often I would actually be walking alone. The Sherpa guide would hike with us for the first hour in the morning, but then take off to scout where we would eat our midday meal. The porters needed to pack the tents and other supplies after we had vacated the premises. Then they would pass us on the way up. Paul was a fairly fast hiker. There was no way I could keep up with his pace. And the truth is, each person must find their pace. If you go too fast, you'll quickly tire. If someone tries to walk slow, it also throws them off. So, in the morning, Paul and I would hike together for the first hour or so. And then Paul would take off on his pace. *I had a lot of time to reflect on life.*

Of course, one is surrounded by stunning mountains and for most of the hike, Ama Dablam was the mountain that rose before me. Turns out Everest isn't that interesting as a visual and you never see it as you're climbing. You still don't see it when you finally get to base camp. Many hikers will climb Kala Patthar, and from this side peak, you get a great view of Everest. In my time alone, I had plenty of time to reflect on my work in India.

First, I considered my work in India on smallpox eradication and how grateful I was to have the opportunity to join WHO and work in the eradication program. As we got closer to the elusive target of zero cases, we gained confidence that this time, we were going to win the battle and that it would be done in a country like India! Everyone thought that India would never be able to gain control over the virus. I realized how lucky I was to be given the chance to even participate in the program because WHO usually only took experts in their fields. And then because of the culture and the caste system, the Indian program had shied away from hiring women. Most Americans who worked in India on smallpox came to the program via the Centers for Disease Control. They usually came for a three-month tour of duty because, at the time, EIS officers were to focus on protecting the health of the USA. However, CDC well understood that in order to protect the USA, you needed to gain experience in new outbreaks. You needed to collect the new viruses or bacteria and take them back to the lab to study. You couldn't just enter a sovereign country. *You had to be invited.* And the way to get invited was to be on a WHO team. So, for CDC epidemiologists to gain expertise and knowledge, they needed to be invited to work with WHO. That's why it's so shortsighted and pig-headed for President Trump to "withdraw the USA from the WHO." Alone, the USA will never be invited to come into a country to evaluate a problem.

So, I was fortunate to get hired by WHO. Dr. Wherle, my pediatric chief at LA County, did a lot of consultancy work for WHO in infectious diseases and was well respected by the organization. When he was writing references for me for my first job out of residency, WHO had sent out feelers for young doctors to work in difficult districts in India. My chief proposed my name to D.A. Henderson, Head of Smallpox Program in Geneva, who was well aware that the Indian program wouldn't be readily accepting female applicants. But Dr. Wherle attested that I would be able to withstand the physical and emotional difficulties of the job. Dr. Wherle had confidence in my ability and put his reputation on the line. Henderson then forwarded my name to India and put his support behind my application. They both took a huge risk not knowing for sure if I could do the fieldwork. I was grateful that the opportunity was offered. I couldn't fail. I hadn't even heard of CDC/Atlanta before being in India. This isn't so far-fetched because if you're committed to clinical work, going into public health wasn't even an option to consider. It wasn't even brought up as something to consider.

I liked smallpox work and international public health. And when Dr. D.A. Henderson came out to India before he retired from WHO and went on to be the Dean of the School of Public Health at Johns Hopkins, he offered me a fantastic opportunity to get in on the ground floor in the newly created WHO Expanded Program of Immunizations. With D.A.'s recommendation, they would have accepted me even given my youth and lack of experience, because I worked and exceled in the highly successful smallpox eradication program. But I trained as a pediatrician and was now confused about what I wanted to do in medicine. Should I give up clinical medicine? I told D.A. I thought I should return to the states and go back to clinical and then decide whether I should change direction.

Walking alone on the Everest trail allowed me to be both vulnerable and open to connecting to others hiking up the trail. If you trek all the time in your "bubble" and circle of friends, you don't need others. My guide and Paul had been waiting for me at the tea house at Lobuche. They were anxious to get hiking up to Gorak Shep, which was where we were going to make camp for the night. Sonnam stressed that I was not to loiter at the tea station. He also underlined that this was *the last place to get water.* There wouldn't be another place on the trail before Gorak Shep.

"Connie, don't stay here long. The climb ahead is still strenuous. Don't forget to fill your water bottle before leaving! There's no water source on the trail." Then they took off up the trail.

I didn't mean to stay more than fifteen minutes at the tea shop. I ordered some tea and gulped it down, but I was really tired. I thought to lie down *just for 10 minutes!* Then someone ripped my hat off while I was lying in the sun on a bench before the tea shop.

I only caught the back of some guy trekker going into the shop. I looked at my watch and I almost had a heart attack. I should have left this place 40 minutes ago. I knew the ascent would be difficult, so I threw on my day pack, and started a fast pace up the mountain. I knew I couldn't keep up this pace, so I slowed down to my usual crawl. And then I realized "Fuck, I forgot to fill my canteen! Damn!" I couldn't retrace my steps. I needed to keep going to get into camp before it got dark. Near the equator, the night falls quickly. But my throat was already parched with thirst. How would I get to Gorak Shep? As I panted beside the trail, I heard footsteps coming up the trail. So, this was the jerk who ripped off my hat, but thankfully, also woke me up.

He stopped on the trail and we introduced ourselves. He took one look at me and offered me his water bottle. He didn't admonish me to "just take a little sip." I think I gulped down half his water. I told him I forgot to fill my canteen at the tea shop. "Thank you for offering me your water."

He said his name was Larry and he would be staying at Gorak Shep. There was a lodge and it was a gathering place for various teams trekking on to Base Camp. Would I be going to the lodge?

I said, "For sure, if I get up the mountain, I'll go to the lodge. You'll get in long before me. If you pass my group, can you tell them that you saw me, that I was on the trail but going slowly?" Larry said he would pass on the word that I was still walking up the trail.

Larry saved my life. I doubt I could have made it up the steep trail without that infusion of water. He didn't have to share. It cut down on his reserve. But he saw a need and he gave unselfishly. Many people would just have nodded and continued up the trail. But he stopped. He had empathy. I thank him to this day! Larry found my group and guide and told them I was plodding up the trail. We met later around the campfire in the lodge with some forty other folk climbing toward base camp. I met Larry later in Kathmandu and we reminisced about the trail and the challenges. I owe him my life. And when I wrote my memoir *Searching for Sitala Mata, Eradicating*

Smallpox in India, I tried to find Larry to ask his consent to be in my memoir but was unsuccessful at the time. Just so you know, *I did find Larry some 43 years later* (June 2019) thanks to FaceBook and LinkedIn. Oh, the power and the ruination of the internet! I just want to leave a thought: *Being alone allows you to plan your life.* Also, I think *"Solitude helps you know yourself."*

Decision Time

❦

YOU SHOULD CAREFULLY weigh solo travel. It isn't something to take up lightly as some "challenge." I think if you analyze the situation carefully, the pros may outweigh the cons. Only you can make that determination. And it shouldn't be made lightly. For me, I needed to get out of my comfort zone. I tried to plan it in the safest way. Things don't always turn out the way you expect. Be ready to take responsibility for your actions. Don't whine and blame others. You make the decision; then you own the decision.

I wanted to see the world as much as possible. I didn't know when or if I would ever return to Asia. The decision was simple: return immediately and find a safe job in California and start doing what you were meant to do. Or, this is a once-in-a-lifetime chance to see this part of the world. Who knew when or if you could ever return? So, you either accept the challenge and see the world or scurry home. I chose to see the world. I chose to explore the opportunity. I gave myself six months to see "the possibilities." This was a window of opportunity not to be missed. So, I went for it. I traveled solo from Kabul to Tehran, to Nairobi, and then on to Europe before heading home. *I've never regretted that choice.*

In an earlier chapter, I urged you to be open to opportunities. Going solo to Kabul turned out to be challenging. I wanted to prove to myself that I could do it alone and then a stalker followed me The basic honesty and hospitality of the Afghan people came to my defense. Yet this run-in with the stalker shook my confidence initially. I met up with Carl in Tehran and saw the cultural sites. Then I went to the airline and found they were stopping this leg of Pan Am. So, I had to scramble to figure out how to get out of Iran and on to Kenya which was my next destination.

I arranged my solo travels so that I would be on my own for a time, but then I hooked up with friends or persons met along the way to gather some "comfort" from being around good friends. For example, before leaving India after my smallpox days, I went up to Kashmir and Ladakh. On the Ladakh trip, I met two French airline hostesses as they were known in those days. But the fourth member of our little tour to Ladakh was Jurgen, a German student. We shared accommodations on the road trip. He invited me to visit him in Berlin so he could show me his city. So, when I left Kenya definitively after the Turkana Bus trip, my next stop was to see Jurgen in Berlin and to visit the au pair Annette K. who lived across the street from me in Jaipur. Her family had a farm on the border with East Germany.

Jurgen was working when I eventually showed up in Berlin. So, during the day, I could revisit old haunts seen from my hitchhiking days when I was a student in Florence. I first appeased my sweet tooth by visiting one of the famous coffee houses that had tantalizing German cakes such as the Black Forest gateaux. I had forgotten how well Germans make coffee. For most of my time in India, I was, by default, from the lack of coffee, a tea drinker. So, I luxuriated in being able to drink great coffee and not the café Americano kind. In the evenings, Jurgen showed me his neighborhood haunts and nightspots. I only stayed for three days because I wanted to also visit my friend Annette who had returned to her family's farm in Versmold.

Traveling was fun, exciting, tantalizing, yet after six months on the road, it can get tiring! I have a love affair with Paris, so I always try to pass by Paris to see the familiar sites. And then on to London for the final goodbye to Europe before heading home to California. Carl showed up in London and we had a wonderful time reliving our adventure along the Hippie Trail. But underlying this and what was ultimately pulling me back to California was that I wanted to practice medicine. I needed to see if clinical medicine spoke to me or international public health. I had to practice medicine to find out.

REMEMBER TO HAVE FUN ALONG THE WAY

A mericans as a society are always being busy. We plan constantly for the future. Or we're looking back on the past and seeing how we could have improved the situation. *Sometimes, we forget to appreciate the moment, to live in the present.* We need to slow down and smell the roses. At the time, it can be difficult to discern if you're always seeking adventure or if you're just being open to the opportunities. It might be a little of both. So, as I reflect on the first half of my life, *I ask my younger self, Did I have fun along the way? Did I make a difference?*

Do You Remember the Very First Time?

🌿

DO YOU REMEMBER the first time you saw snow? Do you remember the thrill of finally mastering the bicycle and staying erect the full length of the block? The smile on your face, the sense of accomplishment, you were bursting with pride and joy! I remember the first-time rappelling down a cliff somewhere in Concord CA with my Girl Scout troop. We had tied on our ropes around our waists and climbed up this short cliff going from handhold to foothold until we were at the top. And then to descend, we belayed on to our partner who was holding the cable. I was looking down over the cliff and you just had to step off into the oblivion. But it was difficult to push off into the unknown. I was scared. I was afraid to step over the edge and go down. I might have stood there for an eternity before being admonished to get going. *Still, once you commit to the first step, the rest is easy.*

How about horseback riding? Do you remember the trot, and learning to stand up and down to find the rhythm? Or getting the horse to go into a smooth canter. It's hard to describe the sense of accomplishment when you finally are one with the horse. It was so much fun with the wind in your hair and the feeling of invincibility! *As one grows older, it is harder to find activities that bring that first thrill, that new excitement, that sense of both independence and vulnerability.* And risking has certain elements of being both: independent but also vulnerable.

Do you remember learning to ski, learning to tumble in judo, learning to swim? You need the desire to learn and the correct instruction, but, overall, you need the will to try. The first attempt may be awkward, stupid, or make you look a fool. But persistence will build confidence and give success. And with success comes an indescribable feeling. Life is to be enjoyed. We need both emotions: to cry with excitement but also to laugh with unrestrained joy.

I remember the first days of being in Florence and listening to the sounds of the city. These sounds were different from those in an American city. The words and shouts outside were in Italian. After the first days, you started to discern a few words: Buon Giorno, ciao. You took tentative steps to explore the streets surrounding your lodging. The first time you go to university, find your class, and then to try to comprehend what the professor was saying was all new and it was exciting. And it was even more exciting to find your way home and know you had mastered your first Italian class at the University. As I passed the flower seller, he stretched out his hand and handed me a single red rose. "Bella, bellisima," he said. And as my cheeks turned red, I glanced back to the stand and gave a huge smile and said, "Gracie, multi gracies." Your first compliment, freely given, gratefully accepted. There would be many other compliments given in Italy, Switzerland, and Germany. Yet it was the people of Italy who showed me how to be open and accept the compliments. And it was fun!

Butter Tea in Lamayuru

❧

I REMEMBER THINKING, *this is almost Tibet!* In my first posting in India working on smallpox eradication, I voraciously read all the memoirs of the British explorers trying to sneak into Tibet. I figured I would never get to see that elusive country, so I jumped at the chance at the end of my stay in India, to go to Ladakh.

Ladakh is a region administered currently by India as a union territory and constituting a part of the larger region of Kashmir, which has been the subject of dispute between India, Pakistan, and China since 1947. The area is still causing controversy and hostilities today. It is bordered by the Tibet Autonomous Region to the east, the Indian state of Himachal Pradesh to the south, both the Indian union territory of Jammu and Kashmir and the Pakistan-administered Gilgit-Baltistan to the west and the southwest corner of Xinjiang across the Karakoram Pass in the far north. Until 2019, Ladakh was a region of the state of Jammu and Kashmir. In August 2019, the Parliament of India passed an act by which Ladakh became a union territory on 31 October 2019.

In the past, Ladakh gained importance from its strategic location at the crossroads of important trade routes, but since the Chinese authorities closed the borders between Tibet Autonomous Region and Ladakh in the 1960s, international trade has dwindled except for tourism. Since 1974, the Government of India has opened the region to tourism. In 1977 while visiting Kashmir, I saw a notice on a houseboat that two women were looking for two others to share an overland trip into Ladakh, a region known as Little Tibet. I jumped at the chance and with a male German student, we four started on the trip. It was early May and one of the snow-covered passes had an avalanche. It took us three attempts to scale and pass over the formidable Zoji La Pass.

The largest town in Ladakh is Leh, followed by Kargil, each of which is the headquarters of a district. Ladakh has a non-Muslim majority. The main religious groups in the region are Muslims (mainly Shia) (46%), Tibetan Buddhists (40%), Hindus (12%), and others (2%). Ladakh is one of the most sparsely populated regions in India. In addition, Ladakh is the largest and the second least populous union territory of India.

Lamayuru is one of the oldest and most famous Buddhist monasteries in Ladakh. The word "Lamayuru" means "eternal" in the Tibetan language; hence, the monastery is known as *the eternal one*. It is situated on the Srinagar-Leh highway 15 kilometers (9.3 mi) east of the Fotu La Pass at a height of 3,510 meters (11,520 ft). It started as an ancient Bon monastery, but, at some stage, it was taken over by the Ka-dam-pa, and when it fell into decline, it was taken over again by the Red Hat sect of Buddhism. When our jeep finally made it over the last pass, we were tired but elated. It was only fitting to stop at the monastery to give thanks for our safe journey and to finally taste real Tibetan butter tea.

We parked, entered the gompa, and were led by a young monk into a side chapel of the monastery. We took off our shoes at the entrance to the chapel and gratefully sank on the cushions before the temple altar. After about ten minutes, an older monk came into the temple with a troop of junior students carrying flasks of hot water, dark brick tea, yak butter, milk, and two antique looking tall, wooden butter urns well worn. I was looking forward to drinking real Tibetan butter tea. When I went to Kathmandu in 1976 to climb to the Base Camp of Mt. Everest, I had several servings of what the Nepalese said was Tibetan tea, but I was doubtful. I knew you had to use yak butter, a very dark tea, and salt.

Tea was introduced to the region as far back as the tenth century, and *po cha* was born less like a ritual and more as a means of survival, making use of the mountain area's available resources: black tea grown in Pemagul, Tibet; butter from the surrounding yaks; and Himalayan salt, the primary flavoring. Tibetan medicine has also long supported the combination of butter and tea as a means of sharpening one's mind and body. Unlike the culture surrounding tea in countries like Japan, complex ceremonies and nuance are practically nonexistent when it comes to po cha; it's a simple, essential drink.

No occasion in Ladakh would be complete without butter tea. It was served during weddings, festivals, and all-important occasions of Ladakh. People of Ladakh drank it all day as it not only provided warmth, but also kept the body hydrated in a cold, high-altitude area. Known as *gur-gur chai*, the tea is prepared with butter, milk, and salt that's added and churned until thoroughly mixed with boiled tea leaves. While butter tea may be straightforward in its ingredient list, it's surprisingly time-intensive to make. Black tea is the base; a special variety from Pemagul is preferred, as it serves as a strong and smoky foundation for the dairy-heavy preparation. A brick of these tea leaves gets steeped for an obscenely long time— until the color becomes almost black. This can take as long as a half day. The tea is then poured into a special bamboo churn about 32 inches tall. A few tablespoons of yak butter, a handful of salt, and sometimes additional milk is added, and the whole drink gets churned like making butter in the old traditional way.

Bulletproof Coffee may be this decade's hottest breakfast craze, but in Tibet, putting butter in your morning beverage is a centuries-long tradition. In the cold, high-altitude conditions of the Himalayan region, the salty, caloric, and energizing po cha—or butter tea—is a daily ritual, forming a large part of the often-sparse Tibetan diet. "Tibet is the highest plateau in the world, so butter tea is like a special kind of oxygen for us," says Tsering Tamding la, a Tibetan chef now based in Oakland, CA. Though regular cow butter is used from time to time to make butter tea, yak butter is most common, as it has a richer, less sweet taste (the result of the Himalayan yak diet, which is very grass and shrub heavy). Aside from the flavor, Tamding la says that yak butter is prized because it signifies "richness, prosperity, and something long lasting" in Tibetan culture.

Alright, I know you want to know "What does it taste like?" The resulting tea looks more like a thick soup than a tea, and it is meant to be consumed as such, in deep bowls that will continually get topped up. As far as the final flavor goes, it can be off-putting at first to taste almost no sweetness. But Tamding la says that this is standard for Tibetans, as the cuisine tends not to be very sweet. "It's like a light soup that's a little salty. It's not that heavy; you don't taste anything like cream or butter. It's just very soothing and rich. In the cold climate, you feel very satisfied."

We still had to get to Kargil, which was even now hours down the road but, technically, we were in the high Ladakhi plateau. We pulled into Kargil as the light was fading, made ourselves eat some Tibetan momos, and then were out like a light. I remember thinking before I fell off to sleep, that our persistence was worth it to get over the landslide. *We had made it to Ladakh!* Sitting in the monastery and watching the monk slowly adding the ingredients into the churn, was like a dream. And then the younger monk was churning the liquid for like 15 minutes. Okay, maybe butter tea is an acquired taste, but I felt I was in another time, an ageless time. This was the real Tibetan butter tea and as I drank the warm liquid, I relaxed and thought, *We did it! We made it over the avalanche. And it was fun! And it was worth all the hassle!*

I didn't know then that I would one day make it to Tibet and Lhasa. It was 38 years later and I would have numerous cups of butter tea there. *Yet I still savor the memory of that first time, of that first sip in Ladakh.*

Delivering My Very First...Calf

❧

I MET ANNETTE in Jaipur when I went to a polo match in the capital (1976). At the time, there weren't many ex-pats who were based in the city. And there were even fewer women ex-pats. So, we spotted each other and introduced ourselves. Although I traveled a lot for my smallpox work, when I was physically in Jaipur, anything to do with horses and cultural events, you would find me there. Annette was an *au pair* (nanny) for a British diplomatic family who had a six-year-old son. She was looking for someone her own age to hang out with. Annette was tall (around 5 ft 8 in) and blond hair, so she was always getting attention. She came from a small town in West Germany and her dad was a dairy farmer. She wanted to see the world, and being an au pair allowed her some independence and freedom.

She had been in Jaipur for almost a year and half, but her British family was waiting for posting to another country. So, she would be leaving shortly. I told her my work was successful in smallpox eradication and that once the country was certified free in May 1977, I also would be leaving India and taking the long way home. She invited me to visit her if I would be going through Europe. I already told Jurgen I would be going through Berlin and Annette said her town wasn't that far. She could drive and pick me up from Berlin. While it was harder to plan things, since this was before cell phones and FaceBook, I could still write and then call once I got to Berlin. So, we left it fluid. She thought it might take a while for her to get another au pair job. I thought that after the fast pace of

163

West Berlin, it might be nice to go to a slower paced rural area just to slow down and relax.

I was excited to see her again and to catch up on our activities since she left India. We caught up on the drive from Berlin to Versmold. Life on the farm wasn't as exciting as Jaipur. None of the men at home were as invigorating as the polo riders in Jaipur. Her parents were getting older and wanted her to settle down. I regaled her with my travels at the end of India, Afghanistan, Iran, and Kenya. They were good travels, but I was getting tired and wanting to get back and working on medicine. So, she didn't need to entertain me; just let me chill.

The life of a dairy farmer isn't easy. You don't have the luxury of sleeping in. I volunteered to help milk the cows at 5 am! The last time I was on a farm was when I was five and there was a tornado that tore through Kansas. Hopefully, we could skip the tornado. Her dad just had to wake me in the morning. I'm a light sleeper, so his gentle nudge was all I needed. Did you know it's dark at 5 am? The cows were already in their stalls. Farmer Jon showed me how to wash the udders. He had already prepared the wash solution. He asked if I knew how to milk manually. "When I was five years old, Farmer Brown showed me in Kansas" I said. Now I had to perform. I took the teats between my hands and slowly pulled down. First one, then the other. On the second try out squirted some milk in the pail. That earned me a congratulatory pat on the back. I really was a milkmaid. Then Farmer Jon showed me how to hook up the teats to a milk machine. This was high tech for me! My task first was to wash down all the udders. And then I could start to hook them up to the machines.

The process went fairly fast. This was a small farm. There were only thirty cows. The milk was collected into a big vat, but Farmer Jon siphoned off some to take into the house. Apparently, someone comes around from the municipality to collect the milk each day around 9 am. The milk that we drank at the farm wasn't pasteurized first, it was just drunk straight as is. But the milk going to the town would be pasteurized before selling. By 7 am, we were heading to the kitchen for a hearty breakfast. Annette's Mom was already there, frying eggs and bacon and the coffee was hot and ready. Annette was still sleeping upstairs.

Once we had finished breakfast, we needed to go back to the barn to take the cows to pasture. The cows knew the procedure. The gate was left open and they just calmly walked into the area. We then closed the gate behind them. Farmer Jon told me that cows are funny, and they can get spooked at any little thing. If they turn around and start to run toward you, *never turn your back and run!* Just stand your ground and put your arms up and they'll stop (usually). One of the cows was heavily pregnant, which I commented on. He was quite proud of this heifer (a female bovine that had not delivered a calf yet). She had been impregnated with some prize bull semen for which he had paid a lot of money to improve his stock. She would be delivering soon, within the week. Wow, I might be able to see an actual birth. That would be a thrilling sight.

We took long country walks in the afternoon, and I was able to read some more of the book I was carrying. I thoroughly enjoyed this bit of leisure, but I could see that the routine would get a little old after a month. The third day, they got a phone call from Farmer Jon's cousin who lived somewhere in East Germany. He had some kind of emergency, so Farmer Jon was going there to bring him some money. I didn't ask too many questions because I knew the border wasn't "open." He was only going for a day and would be home late that night. Maria, his wife, said, "Don't worry, we girls can take care of everything. The calf isn't due for another couple of days." And off he went.

We had slightly more chores since Farmer Jon wasn't there and after lunch I was looking forward to a nice nap. I had just laid down when I heard a commotion in the kitchen. Maria was talking excitedly with Annette. Annette ran up the stairs to my room and said, "The pregnant cow is starting to have contractions early. My Mom is worried."

"But why is she worried?" I asked. "I thought cows just delivered the calf by themselves." Annette explained that usually, that's the case. It's just that, in this case, with the special impregnation, her Mom didn't want any problems.

"Are you going to help with the birth?" I asked.

Annette shook her head and said, "Blood makes me queasy so I'm not going near the barn."

"Well, maybe I should go down to help your Mom," I said. *Not that I've ever delivered a calf,* I thought.

When I got back to the barn, I found Maria with the cow in a special stall in another section. The cow was on her side laying down and panting. Maria looked up with a worried frown and explained that she thought the calf was too large, and the cow was having difficulty pushing it out. "I've delivered about 100 human babies, but I don't know what to do with a cow." Maria went to get some birth implements. There were fresh clean towels to dry off the calf. Maria carried in a strange tool that was shaped like a wooden bow. There was also a length of rope. She slipped on a long glove and entered the cow's vulva. She said, "the calf is positioned correctly, and the forelegs are straight and positioned well. The calf is just too large. We'll have to pull it out. "What do you mean by we?" I asked. She slipped her arm back in with the rope to tie around the front two hoofs. And then she attached the rope to the two ends of the wooden puller. Maria was a little woman, not quite 5 ft tall, and slight. She positioned me at the back squatting and holding the "calf extractor." She showed me how to apply traction. Then she went around to the abdomen and started massaging the belly and waiting to feel for a contraction. Once she felt it, she told me to pull steadily. I was straining with all my might when, suddenly, there was a gush of amniotic water and blood and I fell backwards on the floor. The calf slid out and on top of me on my chest. Maria quickly opened its mouth, removed any mucous, and sprinkled some meds into its nose that made it sneeze and start to breathe. Then she started to towel dry the calf. She slipped off the rope around the front hoofs and then laid the calf on the fresh hay.

It all happened so quickly I was still lying on the hay on the floor completely sopping wet with amniotic fluid and blood. But I was so happy the calf was breathing. "Is everything all right?" I asked. The cow was still lying down but not panting anymore. Birth is still this wonderful miraculous thing. The calf was sitting on folded legs but would be standing in two hours. "Why don't you go and take a shower, suggested Maria. You did a great job! I'm so glad you were here to assist." I was exhausted. I stood in the shower for a good 30 minutes, rewinding the scene in my head. I just helped deliver a calf. And thank God it's alright. *Well, now I can put that on my resume!* **But I forgot to look to see if it was a girl or a boy.**

There Is Still Time to
Do What You Want

❧

LIFE IN THE time of Covid-19. The year started normally. I was still reveling in the knowledge that I got back from Bhutan in November 2019 in just the nick of time! The government had opened up the remote eastern and central areas of the country that were still untouched by hordes of tourists. It's a sad fact but true that tourists gain so much from travel and partaking in time-honored traditions that have stayed the course for millennia. But one has to ask, exactly what do those isolated communities gain from us? We introduce new people, new material things like iPhones, and computers. We may have warmer down jackets, and we obviously have money. Anyone would be attracted to these new items. But it sets up a desire to have more, to leave a mundane existence and go for the bright lights. Desire can lead to envy, to want, to change, to dissatisfaction, and eventually to unhappiness. I wanted to see eastern Bhutan while it was still "pristine." And on my way home to Mexico, I stopped in Kathmandu to arrange how I wanted to leave this place called earth. When I worked in Asia and especially in India, I was attracted to Buddhism and I started to incorporate many of the tenets of the Buddhist way of life.

I wanted at the end of life to have some Buddhist monks chant the funeral rites of the Dead and to light 108 candles to help me pass into the next life. I figured I shouldn't let my daughter be stuck in figuring out how this was to be done, so I had to do the investigation. Besides, I was so close to Nepal, I thought it's highly unlikely that I would pass this way again. I had many great memories of India and Nepal and why not do a sort of "farewell tour"? So, with the help of my guide, I met the Head Lama at Boudhanath temple and was able to lay out how Romene, my daughter, could easily carry out my wishes: to carry my ashes to Boudhanath and for the monks to chant my way to the next life.

I was back in Mexico for Christmas 2019, but my daughter was taking advantage of traveling to London and Paris revisiting those cities and seeing friends from college while she was still young. I traveled to Europe when I was young, and that was exactly the time to travel (when you can partake of its treasures at 28 rather than 70!). She still visited me later during the four-day Martin Luther King holiday in January 2020. So, life was good. And then the world was hit with a new disease coming out of the "wet markets" of Wuhan, China. The United States wasn't prepared for this new novel virus. The world wasn't prepared for this virus. And the U.S. federal government had a recalcitrant, narcissistic president who could only think about his reelection. I'm now starting my eighth month in semi-isolation of my choosing, trying to keep myself healthy. I suppose I was more prepared than most to face a novel pandemic, since I worked as one of those *Disease Detectives* trained by the illustrious Centers for Disease Control and Protection in Atlanta. And it was true that I worked in the famous Smallpox Eradication Program in India with the WHO, helped stamp out the H1N1 Avian Influenza outbreak in East Africa, and made my living addressing resistant malaria in Cambodia and other countries in Africa and Asia. I worked on more infectious diseases than I care to remember, all save one: Ebola! I was retiring just as Ebola was rising. I had a bad feeling about Ebola. My intuition told me to retire. I didn't want to push my luck. So, I did retire!

Now with the beauty of hindsight, I came to think of life in two dimensions: Pre-COVID-19 and Post-COVID-19; even though we haven't reached the post-COVID-19 time. In life, I had to act as if I were an extrovert due to my various positions as Director of Health and infectious diseases advisor. But in the Leadership Training that I attended in Colorado, when given the Briggs-Myers test, it turns out I'm deeply introverted. Even so, in this time of isolation, I find I'm drifting. It turns out that even the most introverted among us are still wired to crave company. It's an *evolutionary imperative* because, historically, there's been safety in numbers. Loners had a tough time slaying the woolly mammoth and fending off enemy attacks.

So, when we're cut off from others, our brains interpret it as a mortal threat. Feeling lonely or isolated is as much a biological signal as hunger or thirst. And just like not eating when you're starved or not drinking when you're dehydrated, failing to interact with others when you're lonely leads to negative cognitive, emotional, and physiological effects, which many of us are likely experiencing now. We underestimated how much we benefit from casual camaraderie at the office, gym, theater, or art class, not to mention spontaneous exchanges with strangers. *Many of us haven't met anyone new in months.*

Daily interacting with individuals out in the world gives you a sense of belonging and security that comes from feeling you're part of or have access to a wider community and network. Social isolation is the kiss of death.

Privation sends our brains into survival mode, which dampens our ability to recognize and appropriately respond to the subtleties and complexities inherent in social situations. Instead, we become hypervigilant and oversensitive.

Studies have shown that the residents who survive best are the ones who continue to communicate with other people, even if it's just through a phone call. The ones who withdraw and don't reach out, do the worst. That's why it's important to block out time every day to connect with others, whether through a socially distanced chat, telephone call, or, at the very least, a thoughtful text. And as we all gradually re-emerge from our confinement and widen our social circles, *don't expect anyone or anything to be the same.* Studies of crew members returning from a polar expedition showed that those who had the greatest difficulty reintegrating were the ones who expected to resume jobs and relationships exactly where they left off.

People inevitably change over time and certainly after something significant, like a pandemic, upends their lives and shakes their confidence in what they thought they knew. Values shift. Personalities alter. None of us are the same. So, give yourself and everyone else a break. Have patience for your own and other people's weirdness. And as we escape from this enforced cocoon, we see that there is time for a "do-over." *We don't have to live with regrets.* It doesn't matter how old you are, there's still time! As Gandalf said, "All we have to decide is what to do with the time that is given to us." While reflecting on what you've done and where you want to go with the time that remains, the following lessons may be instructive:

Lesson 1: *Forgiveness doesn't equal consent.* Humans often approach forgiveness as something to be bestowed or withheld. Maybe, we should substitute human conflict-resolution methods. After a conflict, what if we pursued reconciliation instead? Within this framework, we identify what made us clash, leave the past behind, and set up new guidelines for how we might treat each other going forward. Researchers suggest reconciliation reduces tension and supports group cohesiveness. *Don't procrastinate.*

Lesson 2: *Meet challenges at your own pace.* Apply the learning: When facing a challenge, many humans apply pressure on themselves to succeed quickly, creating self-inflicted stress. Instead, learn to honor your own pace just as I had to honor my pace as I climbed to the Base Camp of Everest. Ask friends to encourage and reassure you along the way.

Lesson 3: *Success requires self-care.* Social media can create helpful support networks, but it also brings forth disparaging opinions. The lead up to the 2020 elections showed how polarized our nation was. What can we learn: While research on the effect of taking a social media vacation varies, *trusting our instincts on self-care is vital to well-being*. Consider these words from Rabbi Zalman Schachter-Shalomi: "The mind is like tofu. By itself, it has no taste. Everything depends on the flavor of the marinade it steeps in." Are you marinating your mind in support or disapproval?

Lesson 4: *No matter how famous you are, it's not really about you.* Everyone is capable of change. What can we learn? Think about the misfortunes in your life. What impact did they have on you? How might they help you support others who are struggling? Can you feel wonder at the world around you, no matter where you are? This is an incredible practice that will help you feel more alive, each time you do it. What can we do to be fully alive in each moment?

One thought to keep: there's still time. You don't have to live with regret!

Acknowledgments

First, I would like to thank my parents who thought that travel was educational. I think they were dismayed at how far I traveled, but they were always supportive.

Then, I want to thank my fellow travelers in crime: the UN and USAID women who worked and lived overseas with me in the many demanding and risky places in Africa and Asia. You always had my back! Thank you!

I also owe a debt of gratitude to my Editor Wayne H. Purdin, Lead Curriculum Editor Grand Canyon University, AZ. He was able to follow my ramblings through different time periods and made sure I stayed coherent.

Finally, I want to thank Richard Clarke who taught the **Essentials of Elderhood** course at Lakeside on the northern shores of Lake Chapala in Jalisco, Mexico. He urged the group members to leave behind a record, a sort of ethical will, of what each one of us had tried to accomplish in our lifetimes. This book is my witness statement.

About the Author

 Dr. Cornelia E. Davis, better known as Connie, is an author, speaker, renowned epidemiologist, and disease detective. Connie was raised in the San Francisco Bay Area, attended Gonzaga University in Spokane WA, and was one of the first Black women admitted to the University of California, San Francisco School of Medicine (1968). After finishing a pediatric residency in Los Angeles, she was hired by the World Health Organization (WHO) to work in the Smallpox Eradication Program in India (1975-77). India was certified free of smallpox in 1977 and the world was declared smallpox free in 1980. This highly successful program changed her medical focus. Davis earned her Masters of Public Health (MPH) degree from Johns Hopkins School of Public Health and went on to work in the Epidemic Intelligence Service (EIS) at the Centers for Disease Control in Atlanta (1979-81). For the next thirty years, she battled disease outbreaks in Africa and Asia for WHO and USAID.

Dr. Davis went on to work on childhood immunizations, malaria, yellow fever, and dengue fever in Cote d'Ivoire, Mali, Liberia, and Senegal. She was sent by WHO to Ethiopia in 1990 to help African Ministries of Health prevent or control outbreaks of meningococcal meningitis. While working in Addis Ababa, she was caught up in the fast-moving civil war and stayed behind as Acting Director of the WHO EPR Centre when UN staff were evacuated to Nairobi.

During these turbulent times, she came in contact with an orphaned three-month-old infant and adopted her daughter, Romene. Connie went on to live and work in twenty African and Asian countries on malaria, TB, HIV/AIDS, and another pandemic, H1N1 Avian Influenza.

As a world traveler, she has worked in or traveled to 97 countries and territories. She currently lives on the northern shores of Lake Chapala near Guadalajara, Mexico.

Can You Help?

circa 1968 UCSF School of Medicine

Thank You for Reading My Book!

I really appreciate all of your feedback, and I love hearing what you have to say.

I need your input to make the next book in this series and any future books better.

Please leave me an ***honest review on Amazon*** letting me know what you thought of the book.

Thanks so much!

Cornelia (Connie) Davis MD, MPH

BRING DR. CORNELIA "CONNIE" DAVIS TO YOUR ORGANIZATION

Dr. Davis is available for speaking engagements. She is an award-winning author, medical consultant, speaker, traveler, and wayfarer.

Her topics include: inspirational, world health issues, intercountry adoption, and traveling to remote destinations. At a recent gathering, participants said, "She took us along on a journey to places that most of us will never experience. We were all captivated and inspired by her adventures. We loved her book." And so will your audiences.

Contact information below:
Email: CorneliaEDavisMD@gmail.com
Author website: www.CorneliaEDavisMD.com

FOLLOW DR. DAVIS ON SOCIAL MEDIA

Facebook: www.Facebook.com/CorneliaEDavisMD
Pinterest: https://www.pinterest.com.mx/corneliaedavis/
Twitter: www.Twitter.com/CEDavisMD

Made in the USA
Las Vegas, NV
04 September 2021